Becoming a Teacher

The Falmer Press Teachers' Library

Fundamentals of Educational Research
Gary Anderson, *McGill University, Canada*

Search and Re-Search:
What the Inquiring Teacher Needs to Know
Edited by Rita S. Brause, *Fordham University, USA* and
John S. Mayher, *New York University, USA*

Doing Qualitative Research:
Circles Within Circles
Margot Ely, *New York University, USA* with Margaret Anzul,
Teri Friedman, Diane Garner and Ann McCormack Steinmetz

Teachers as Researchers:
Qualitative Inquiry as a Path to Empowerment
Joe L. Kincheloe, *Clemson University, USA*

Key Concepts for Understanding Curriculum
Colin Marsh, *Secondary Education Authority, Western Australia*

Beginning Qualitative Research:
A Philosophic and Practical Guide
Pamela Maykut and Richard Morehouse, *Viterbo College, USA*

The Falmer Press Teachers' Library: 7

Becoming a Teacher:
An Inquiring Dialogue for the Beginning Teacher

Gary D. Borich

 The Falmer Press

(A member of the Taylor & Francis Group)
Washington, D.C. • London

| USA | The Falmer Press, Taylor & Francis Inc., 1900 Frost Road, Suite 101, Bristol, PA 19007 |
| UK | The Falmer Press, 4 John Street, London WC1N 2ET |

First published in 1995

A catalogue record for this book is available from the British Library

Library of Congress Cataloging-in-Publication Data are available on request

ISBN 0 7507 0264 8 cased
ISBN 0 7507 0265 6 paper

Jacket design by Caroline Archer

The sketches drawn by Gabriel Davila, student, Travis High School, Austin, Texas.

Typeset in 12/14pt Bembo by
Graphicraft Typesetters Ltd., Hong Kong

Printed in Great Britain by Burgess Science Press, Basingstoke on paper which has a specified pH value on final paper manufacture of not less than 7.5 and is therefore 'acid free'.

Contents

Sketches

Sketches of young journalist:

Introduction

This story describes some of what has been learned from effective teachers.

By 'effective' I mean how teachers like yourself have helped their students to learn, managed their classrooms better, and felt good about themselves.

This story is a summary of what effective teachers have learned the hard way — from experience — and have passed on to beginning teachers. It reveals some of the behaviors that have made them effective — not only in their own eyes but in those of their students, colleagues and principals.

I hope you will enjoy using what you learn from this story and become a better, more effective teacher as a result of it.

Gary Borich
October, 1994

Part I:

What is an Effective School?

1   The Search for an Effective School

In a city not so very far from yours and mine, there was a journalist who wanted to write a story about teachers. She had heard and read so much that was critical of schools and teachers that she wanted to write a different kind of story. She wanted to write about *effective* schools and about *effective* teachers.

Her search for a story took her many months and to many different places. She visited schools, both small and large, in neighborhoods both rich and poor. She spoke with principals and assistant principals, teachers and teacher aids, and even with some students, both young and old. She went into every corner of the schools she visited and into every grade and content area. She was beginning to see the variety of life in schools.

She saw many 'well organized' schools that were letter perfect but whose teachers seemed ineffective and demoralized. From plaques on the walls she learned that others had come to these schools and given them awards and certificates to recognize their achievements. Why, she did not know.

As she visited some of these 'well organized' schools, she talked with their principals. She asked them, 'What kind of a principal would you say you are?' Their answers varied little.

'I'm a tough-minded principal — I keep on top of things', one said. Others described themselves as: 'organized', 'goals-based', or 'results-oriented'. She could tell from the pride in their voices that these principals were satisfied with themselves.

She also talked with many 'nice' principals — the kind that are instantly liked by their teachers and staff. Many who knew these principals thought they were effective, too. As she sat and listened to these 'nice' principals, she heard a similar story.

'I'm democratic', one said. While others used the words 'supportive', 'understanding' and 'humanistic' to describe themselves and their schools. She could tell from the pride in their voices that these principals, too, were satisfied with themselves. But, she was troubled.

It was as though most principals were either interested in *results* or in *people*. The principals who were interested in results often referred to themselves as 'organized' and those interested in people as 'democratic'. As she thought about each of these types of principals — the 'organized' and the 'democratic' — she wondered if they were only partially effective, like being half of something. Effective principals, she thought, should be both people-oriented *and* results-oriented.

The journalist looked everywhere for an effective school — one that would be both people-oriented *and* results-oriented. She began to worry that there may not be any and that she might have to abandon her story.

But, just as she was about to give up her search, she heard stories about a school that had an effective principal. She heard stories that teachers liked to work for this principal and that together they produced great results. The journalist wondered if the stories were true and decided to visit the principal to see for herself.

She called the principal to ask if she could talk about the stories she had heard about this school. She explained that she was not a teacher, but wanted to know, if it were possible to be an effective teacher and work in an effective school. The principal agreed to see her the very next day.

When she arrived she told the principal that she had heard things about her school that led her to believe that it was an effective school and that there were stories circulating in the district of how much her teachers enjoyed teaching there. She said this was puzzling because in coming there she noticed that the neighborhood was not very good and that the school was, she paused, . . . not as she had expected.

The principal nodded in a way that told her she had heard that same sort of puzzlement before.

The journalist then asked how her school got the reputation for effectiveness it has with students from such a low income neighborhood, and with older, outdated facilities.

The principal responded, 'It's because I'm here to get results. By being well organized, we can achieve some things other schools can't.'

'Oh, so your school is results-oriented', she asked.

'No, not just results-oriented', the principal responded. 'How do you think I get results if I'm not understanding and considerate of those who work for me.'

This puzzled the girl, since it seemed difficult to be both 'hard nosed' enough to get results and considerate and understanding at the same time. So, she asked the principal how she balanced these two very different approaches.

'I'll tell you.'

The principal leaned toward her and asked: 'when do you work at your best?'

She thought for a moment and then answered, 'When I'm excited about what I'm doing.'

Exactly, said the principal, and how do you make a whole school excited about what they're doing?

'I'm not sure', she answered.

Well, let me tell you the things that make a school an exciting place to be.

Reflections

1 Picture a principal who is 'organized', 'goals-based' and 'results-oriented'. Describe how you think his or her school might be run.

2 Now, picture another principal who is 'supportive', 'understanding' and 'humanistic'. Describe how you think his or her school might be run. What differences would you expect to find between this school and the one above?

3 Do you believe the two types of schools you have just described have to be mutually exclusive? Provide some examples within a school of how they could be combined in complementary ways.

4 Place an 'X' in the appropriate quadrant below that best describes the climate of your high school, as you remember it. Then, list some of the things that made your school's climate what it was?

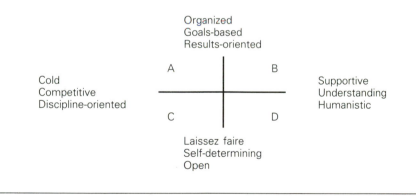

_____

_____
_____
_____

Field Activity

Think of an example of each of the four climates listed below from among the schools and/or classrooms you remember. Then, indicate in the boxes the characteristics or conditions that gave each school or classroom the climate you observed.

1 Organized, goals-based, results oriented climate:

2 Supportive, understanding, humanistic climate:

3 Laissez faire, self-determining, open climate:

4 Cold, competitive, discipline-oriented climate:

Do you believe the climate of a school influences the classrooms within it?

2   The Role of Positive Expectations

The principal began '. . . the longer you teach the more you realize that kids in school have far more in common than they have differences. In this school every teacher starts out at the beginning of the year with a glass that's half full, not half empty.'

'What do you mean?'

'I mean that our teachers have the attitude that every student can learn — that each comes to school with plenty of potential to learn whatever he or she wants to learn. It's our job to help them reach that potential.'

'But, surely your teachers can't expect to do that for everyone, regardless of ability?'

'I'm afraid so. Now, I know what you're thinking — that IQ and ability have a lot to do with how much we learn. And, that some learners have more than others.'

'Yes, that's exactly what I'm thinking.'

'And, in a sense, you're right. We do see differences in intelligence in school in lots of ways — in the commitment to learn, the subjects students choose to study, and in their individual interests. But, those things don't have much to do with what goes on *in* school.'

'I'm not sure I follow.'

'The way I see it, every kid has about the same potential to learn — and a lot of it too. It's just that the focus of that potential for one learner may be different than for another.'

'For example?'

'For example, every learner can become an expert — really accomplished at something. Now, for some that might mean choosing from among becoming an engineer, draftsman or carpenter. For others, it might mean choosing from among becoming a physician, business executive or salesperson. Now, there may be a difference in abilities there, but that difference so happens not to be relevant to what we do *in* school.'

'It isn't?'

'These are choices made by the learner. What we do in this school is nurture the potential to learn — and that means help each student become a success in whatever *they* chose.'

'Do you mean that the students in this school can be successful in any thing they wish?'

'No. I'm saying they can be successful *learners* and that each can succeed as a learner. They may not, by their own choice, be equally successful as a schoolteacher, mailman, chemist or truck driver — which will involve their abilities and how they choose to use them. Only they can be responsible for success in what they choose to become. What we are responsible for is teaching them *how to learn.*'

'Are you saying that you can teach anyone to learn?'

'That's right.'

'Then why do some students take different subjects than others? Isn't that taking into account differences in their abilities?'

'If you'd like to see it that way, but that's not why some students are taking different subjects than others. In this school any student can take any subject they wish, if they are adequately prepared. Our goal is not to teach every student the same subjects, but to teach every student how to learn and to see that every student gets the same *opportunity to learn*. It so happens that the most productive avenue for teaching some students how to learn may involve subject X while the most productive avenue for another student may involve subject Y. Both are *learning to learn* in their own chosen ways and that is the single most important goal in this school.'

'Are you saying that you expect every student in this school to learn how to learn?'

'That's it. It's not that our students will all learn the same things or even that they will learn them to the same degree — that may depend on many things including their interests and abilities. What each student will acquire is an understanding of how to learn — its challenges and discipline as well as its joys and benefits. That's more important than what or how much is learned, since it *allows the learner to choose* what and how much he or she wants to learn.'

'You mean it's something that determines everything else.'

'You bet. And, it's what allows intelligent choices to be made. Without it, even the very brightest couldn't make the choice we so often associate with ability — which is perhaps why some young people today seem unable to become interested in their own future. They simply may never have learned how to learn, enabling them to choose what they want out of life.'

'So, you have the same standard for everyone when it comes to learning.'

'Yes, and our teachers communicate that to every student the very first day of school. Everyone in this school is committed to filling the glass full — to teach each and every student how to learn with whatever methods and resources it takes to get the job done. Our very first task is to make our students more proficient learners and it is that goal for which we have the same high standards and expectations for everyone.'

'But, how do you do that in a school like this with students who have so many different learning needs?'

'Take a moment and look out the window and tell me what you see.' (*She moves toward the window and looks silently for a minute.*)

'I see kids, lots of them, all very different.'

'Do you want to know what *I* see?'

'What?'

'*I* see the *potential to learn.*'

Reflections

1   Using a personal experience, describe a specific instance in your life when you discovered how to learn something. How was this different than 'how much you learned?'

2   Do you believe that teaching every student how to learn requires that some students be taught different subjects than others? What might be some evidence in support of and against this belief?

3   Imagine two schools: one in which everyone has the opportunity to take any subject, and another in which the opportunity to learn some subjects depends on one's intelligence and prior curriculum? Which school would you prefer to attend and why?

4   Describe the difference between a *school* and a *climate for learning*. What characteristics of a school do you believe create a positive climate for learning?

Field Activity

In the boxes below provide some examples of school characteristics you have observed that *foster* a climate for learning how to learn and that *discourage* a climate for learning how to learn.

School characteristics I have observed that foster a climate for learning how to learn:

School characteristics I have observed that discourage a climate for learning how to learn:

3   Focus on Learning

'How do you create a school that gives students the potential to learn?'

'It begins with planning the school day in ways that protect the time teachers have to teach.'

'You mean that's something you have to protect?'

'You bet. Teachers lead hectic lives — meetings to attend, announcements to read, forms to fill out, parents to call — all on top of the time that must be devoted to teaching. That tells you a lot about how difficult it can be to keep a school on track — keeping the train on its tracks and headed in the right direction.'

'So, how do you do it? . . . I mean help your teachers keep the train on the tracks and headed in the right direction?'

'The answer to that comes when you realize that anyone who runs a school like this — or any school — has to have two faces — like the mythical figure, Janus — who could look both ways.'

'Now, some principals might think that one face has to look "up" to central administration and another "down" to teachers. But, what happens with that type of thinking is that you look in only one direction at a time, where your most immediate concern is.'

'So, I stopped thinking of it as looking "up" or "down" but rather — as looking two ways at once.'

'But, isn't that like trying to serve two masters at the same time?'

'Not when both masters have the same goal. You see, both want the train to stay on its tracks and headed in the right direction. My job is to see to it that the engineers, conductors, and station masters can get the passengers to their destination. The school district has to see that there is a train to ride, filled with enough fuel for a long journey and good, safe tracks to ride on. So, a job like mine has to keep one eye on the tracks ahead to be sure there are no obstacles on the way to our destination and one

eye behind to see that everything needed to make the passengers comfortable in their journey is provided. No one is arguing about the need to stay on the track — the question is how to do it in today's hectic world of paperwork and distractions.'

'So, then, how do you do it?'

'Well, I'll tell you. I have to arrange this school in ways that minimize disruptions that take time away from teaching.'

'For example?'

'For example, we have school-wide rules that are given to each student to take home the very first day. These help both students and parents know exactly what will be expected, so they don't need to bother our teachers asking about "why this" or "why that". Parents need to know what's expected of their children — the same as the children need to know. This cuts down on a lot of misunderstandings later when some action that may be unpleasant has to be taken. It's all spelled out in advance.'

'I also have to protect a teacher's time by avoiding interruptions or competing responsibilities that interfere with a teacher's planning time. Every department head and subject area coordinator in this school knows that that's the teacher's time — it's not mine and it's not theirs.'

'So, that's how you focus on learning?'

'That's not all. Some of our most talented and motivated students are asked to assist teachers by helping them with their instructional preparations, such as preparing handouts, passing out materials, writing assignments on the board, and tutoring. These things may seem small, but they're the kinds of things that can wear a teacher down. If they don't directly rob you of instructional time, they can exhaust and overwhelm you before instruction even begins. So, to give our teachers more time to prepare — and to teach — we've organized a dedicated staff of students — we call them teachers' assistants — who are made to feel a part of the instructional staff of the school. Many of these students are looking for just such adult-like responsibilities to help them in the transition between school and their careers.'

'So, it's that simple?'

'Keeping a focus on learning also involves a lot of other things — like how to handle discipline problems that minimize disruptions to the class, establishing fair but effective classroom rules, creating procedures for handling routine interruptions, and using workbooks, supplementary materials and special resources for providing instruction to learners who may be above or below grade level. These are some of the things that a teacher can do to minimize the kinds of distractions and interruptions that can make a classroom look more like the inside of a train station where everybody is standing around waiting to go somewhere than a train that's on the right track and heading toward its destination.'

'Are there any other things that create a focus on learning?'

'There are, but I have some appointments now. Let's save that for another time.'

With that she politely thanked the principal. On the way home, she began to sketch an outline of her story, but realized there was much more she would need to know. She couldn't help but think about whether a school really was like a train — maybe like the one she was riding on — stopping at different stations to accommodate the individual destinations of each of its passengers but always clinging to the same track with a destination understood by all on board.

Anxious to find out what other things this principal would tell her, she called for another appointment. The principal seemed pleased to have her return and arranged a time to meet.

Reflections

1 Describe some of the things you learned from this dialogue that a teacher and principal can do together to establish a focus on learning.

2 Suppose you have to make an important rule about discipline in the classroom. Pose a rule indicating that you have 'looked two ways at once'. Whom did you consider in making your rule?

3 What are some of the responsibilities of a principal in keeping the train on the track and headed in the right direction? What might be some of your responsibilities as a teacher?

4 How valid do you feel it would be to have a school headed for only one destination?

Field Activity

Describe in the box below the things you have noticed teachers do to avoid interruptions or manage competing responsibilities that interfere with their instructional time.

Indicate in the box below the things you think could be but are not always done in the school and classroom to increase a teacher's instructional time.

4   Assessing Learner Progress

'I've thought a lot about the things you've said and I'm a bit puzzled.'

'By what?'

'I was wondering if a school is really like a train moving in one direction. Even a train stops at different stations, which means the people riding the train have different destinations. Some get off at the first stop while others go on to the end of the line. It seems not everyone is heading for the same place and that seems to complicate things.'

'You're right. Not everyone is heading for the same place. In schools as well as trains some go farther than others. But, you're forgetting that I didn't say a school is like a train because everyone wants to arrive at the same *destination*. What I said was that everyone in them — schools as well as trains — want to go in the same *direction*. That's an important distinction.'

'I'm still not sure — destination or direction — what's the difference?'

'An important one. The direction in which schools must be going is to help learners realize their potential to learn. That means filling up the other half of that glass we talked about last time.'

'I'm still not sure I understand.'

'Look at it this way. No one can discover who they really are, what they can become, or even what they want to be without the skills and competencies needed to find one's own way in the world. Those skills and competencies are the vehicles for discovering who we are.'

'Do you mean schools don't really make you into who you are — but give you what you need to discover who you are?'

'They help you change and grow as your situation or the conditions around you change.'

'So, you're saying that every school must provide each passenger on the train with the ability to change and to grow?'

'There is no more important goal. We need only pick up the

newspaper to see that. What we learned yesterday already has become obsolete today and, so, we must continually grow into what we must become tomorrow.'

'So, that's why schools must equip learners to learn how to learn — so they can continually adapt to a life of change.'

'That's right. The failure to be able to step onto the next rung of the learning ladder has bitter consequences, not just for those who "slip and fall", but for all of us who must pay the costs of picking them up.'

'That explains the similarity between the direction of a school and a train, but what about all the stops along the way. Are those the rungs of the learning ladder?'

'Schools have to prepare everyone to negotiate rungs on the ladder — and that means the less able as well as able, the disadvantaged as well as advantaged, the non native as well as native speaker. They are learning in school to negotiate the rungs of the learning ladder by acquiring certain skills that later can assist them to go to any rung his or her heart desires and abilities permit.'

'So, does that mean that schools aren't necessarily supposed to get you to the next rung — but to give you what you need to get there?'

'Schools get you started — and they must get everyone started regardless of background or ability — otherwise they've failed. But, that's different than saying school will place you on the next rung of the ladder. That, I'm afraid, the learner must do for himself or herself — with the help of what is taught in school.'

'So that's how schools have the same direction but the individuals within them can have different destinations — like passengers on the train who are heading in the same direction but getting off at different places along the way to suit themselves.'

'And, one jumping off point is not necessarily better than another. Success or even personal satisfaction may not be achieved any more at one stop than another . . . that all depends on the individual.'

'But each stop does indicate the unique interests and abilities of the passengers.'

'That's right.'

'I think you're talking about life, not just schools. Any other characteristics of an effective school?'

'Another characteristic of an effective school is how well it measures student progress.'

'You mean tests?'

'Not exactly. Formal tests that measure student achievement are part of it — but not the only part. That's where some schools go wrong in my opinion. They test believing that formal assessments can capture *all* that it takes to move learners to the next rung of the learning ladder. But, the truth is that what it takes to get to the next rung of the ladder is very often not knowledge of formal content, which so often is the focus of paper and pencil tests, but the decision-making and problem-solving skills that must be fueled by this knowledge.'

'What I'm saying is that sometimes formal tests don't do a very good job of measuring what it takes to deal with change and adapt your thinking to the world around you. Tests of knowledge or even how to apply it represent *vertical* learning — how well you can move up or down the curriculum from the easier to the more complex stuff. Most of what it takes to move to the next rung of the learning ladder involves *lateral* learning — or the ability to move across the curriculum and across different subjects that may reveal relationships and patterns among subject matter that are useful for decision-making and problem-solving. These are tough to measure with multiple choice, short answer, or even essay questions. Many times they can only be assessed through student *performance.*'

'You mean things like class discussion and oral assignments?'

'Yes, but not just those. Extended writing assignments, creative projects, scientific investigations, oral and written productions, descriptions of work accomplishments, demonstrations, and even one-on-one conversations between teacher and student can also be used for this purpose. These types of assessments more *authentically* represent life experiences and draw students out of the stereotypic behavior sometimes expected by formal tests. Every teacher in this school is expected to provide frequent opportunities for each student to perform in these ways as well as on tests — which *together* are used to measure a learner's progress.'

'So your teachers are expected to do less testing than teachers at other schools.'

'You probably would find the same amount of testing here as anywhere else. What you would find different is the number of entries in a teacher's gradebook that record the results of problem-solving and decision-making in real world contexts, such as class discussions, oral reports, critical analyses before the class, extended projects, and one-on-one dialogues in which the student is expected to orally express and model putting his or her knowledge and skill to work in some practical way.'

'And, wouldn't all that change the way a teacher teaches? I mean wouldn't the teacher present things differently to bring out these problem-solving and decision-making skills?'

'That's exactly where the train should be heading. These problem-oriented and decision-making behaviors are what we should be after in the long run — they're what get students onto the next rung of the learning ladder faster and allow students to think laterally — make associations, discover patterns, and find relationships — just the type of thinking you and I do everyday in our adult lives. And, it should provide more and better feedback to students as to where *they* should be going. That's what keeps the train on the track — consistent and frequent assessment of student progress that can tell both teacher and student what has to happen next.'

'Is there anything else you can tell me about what makes a school effective?'

'There is, but I'm afraid we'll have to leave that for another visit.'

She took the next week to think about the things the principal had said and what she might write about. While much of it, she thought, made sense — it seemed too simple — like commonsense that required nothing new or even anything very complicated. Nothing truly effective could be that simple and, so, there, she thought, is where she would begin her questioning the next time.

Reflections

1   Describe in your own words how a school might be like a train heading in one direction but accommodating passengers with different destinations. In what ways might a school be unlike a train?

2   In your discipline or grade level what would be some important 'rungs of the learning ladder' that you would feel responsible for?

3   How do authentic assessments of learning differ from traditional paper and pencil tests? Provide some original examples in your subject or grade of performance assessments.

4   What is the purpose of lateral as opposed to vertical learning? Why do we need both? How might both be taught within a single lesson or unit?

Field Activity

From your experience, identify in the boxes below some examples of vertical and lateral learning in a classroom. Describe how different bodies of knowledge might be integrated in a single lesson or unit with the concept of lateral learning.

Examples of vertical learning:

Examples of lateral learning:

5   Teacher Participation and Team Decision-making

'You've told me that this school is different than some other schools because it has *positive expectations for its students, a focus on learning, and assessments of student progress that require decision-making and problem-solving skills.*'

'That's right.'

'You will have to excuse me for asking but these things seem so simple — commonsense you might say — that if they truly make a difference, wouldn't every school be doing them?'

'Well, first of all these aren't the only things we do differently that makes this school effective. There's more to it — but you're right, they are commonsense — like the kind of things you might do in raising your own family, running a successful business, or planning a vacation. That's why they aren't new. People — successful people — have been doing them for a long time.'

'So, why doesn't every school do these things, since, as you say, they aren't new?'

'Because commonsense notions like having positive expectations for students of all ability levels, actively providing a focus on learning during a hectic school day and authentic assessments of student progress that get at decision-making and problem solving skills don't mean much until you discover them for yourself.'

'You mean you can't learn about them before you experience them.'

'Oh, you can learn about them from textbooks and workshops — but you can't really *understand* them until you discover them for yourself. They might get you an "A" on a test but they won't change your life.'

'I'm not sure I follow.'

'You're wondering why all schools don't do these things.'

'That's right.'

'Because some have simply memorized a list of what it means to be effective — you know — like cramming for a test to get an "A". They haven't taken the time to understand, really experience I mean, what's on the test. I would give most schools an "A" for being able to say what it takes to be effective. As you say, that part's commonsense — and this commonsense has been written about so often that every principal worth his or her salt could recite it by heart.'

'And, so, what's wrong with that?'

'Well, the problem I'm getting at is the same one we have in teaching Johnny to read. Johnny doesn't really read — I mean understand what he's read — until he, in some sense, discovers it for himself. Oh, he can learn vocabulary and memorize what he's read and maybe even get an "A" by giving it back to you. But, that doesn't mean he'll remember it for very long and it doesn't mean he can use this new skill to solve problems and make decisions in the real world. That's because he may have been only a *recipient* and not a *participant* in the learning process. And that brings me to my next point and I think the answer to your question.'

'I was hoping you'd get to that.'

'The key to what I've been saying is that no matter what may appear to be commonsense, it will do no good unless you discover it for yourself. In other words, no one can really teach it to you — at least so you truly understand it and can use it in your own daily life. That's why commonsense isn't so very common. It's there, but it's not there. The minute you think you have it memorized, it evaporates before your eyes, gets forgotten — unless you've had the chance to experience it.'

'So, what you're saying is that schools should be set up so that students *experience* what they're learning.'

'Yes, by using what is learned to solve problems and make decisions — real ones, not just those at the end of the chapter but ones that go beyond the text and workbook — that bridge the gap between the classroom and the world outside.'

'But, how can this make a whole school effective?'

'What we've been saying about learning in the classroom applies to the kind of learning that has to go on to make a whole school effective.'

'You mean teachers and administrators have to learn what an effective school is.'

'I would say they have to *experience* it, because most already know what an effective school is. Only by experiencing it do you understand enough to make it an effective school — that is, be able to use what you know to solve real life problems and make decisions that actually make the school better.'

'And so how do you go beyond knowledge to experience how that knowledge can be used to solve problems and make decisions?'

'Now, we've come to the point in which I have to answer your question. Many schools are neither effective nor ineffective but rather they are in the process of discovering what being effective means — converting their *knowledge* of effectiveness into an *understanding* of it.'

'And, how do they do that?'

'In the same way a teacher would get Johnny to understand not just memorize what he's reading.'

'Well, if I've heard you correctly, she'd have to get him to be a *participant* in the learning process not just a *recipient*. And, I guess that would mean involving him in the process of reading by getting him to solve problems and make decisions on his own — with the knowledge of what he's read.'

'That's right. So, now tell me how that same idea could make a whole school more effective and you will have another characteristic of an effective school.'

'I see why it took so long to answer my question. You wanted me to discover some things for myself.'

'And, what have you discovered?'

'Everyone has to participate to make a school effective.'

'Now you see why some schools aren't as effective as they could be. Positive expectations, a focus on learning and authentic assessments of student progress just hang there collecting cobwebs like so many other pronouncements of goodwill without the active participation of its teachers.'

'And, how do you get teachers to participate in making their school effective?'

'That's a big part of my job. It means involving teachers in deciding how this school can be made more effective and giving them the authority to do it through problem-solving and decision-making of their own.'

'So, that's where the ideas of participation and problem-solving come together?'

'That's right. You don't learn — and by that I mean understand — if you're not at the center of a problem. Who wants to be at the center of a problem if you don't have the authority to decide how to solve it? That's where I come in. I provide the administrative leadership that gives others the authority to become leaders. This school is organized by problems — discipline problems, curriculum problems, resource problems, parent and family problems, and even administrative problems. Every teacher in this school serves as a member of a team that considers the problems we have in one or more of these areas. And, with my input and guidance, the decisions that are made are theirs. You'd be surprised how quickly problems are resolved when the teachers themselves are part of the decisions that can make the problems go away.'

'Now I see that without the participation of teachers in making a school effective none of the other characteristics we've talked about would make sense. You're saying that nothing would really happen to change things unless the teachers themselves participated in the changes. I think this is starting to make an interesting story that hasn't been written.'

Reflections

1 In your own words, describe the difference between something that has been *learned* and something that has been *understood*. What would be an example from your own experience of each of these? What would be an example of each from your teaching field?

2 Describe an occasion in which you have been a *recipient* but not a *participant* in the learning process. How could the situation have been turned around to make you a 'participant'?

3 How would you explain to someone why 'commonsense' is not always so common? How do effective teaching practices become 'common'?

4 Describe some of the ways you would have teachers experience and discover for themselves the concept of an effective school.

Field Activity

Talk with a teacher about his or her role in the decision-making process within their school. Record in the box below some of the ways he or she is a *participant*, as opposed to *recipient*, in decisions affecting the entire school. If the teacher has only been a recipient of decisions affecting the school, indicate some of the reasons why and how this situation could be turned around.

6   The Role of Parent and Community Support

Some time passed before she made another appointment. There was a lot to digest before beginning to write her story and she wanted to be confident she understood all that was said. And, still there were many unanswered questions — like how the teachers actually taught in this school, how they managed their classrooms and how they moved their learners to the next rung of the learning ladder. It was to these and other questions she must eventually find answers.

'You said at the end of my last visit how important it was for teachers to participate in the decision-making process of a school — to *experience* not just learn about what made a school effective.'

'That's right.'

'Are there any other characteristics of an effective school?'

'Well, there's one that goes along with that. It's the role of *parent* participation.'

'You mean parents participating in school activities — like the PTSA and back-to-school nights — things like that?'

'That's not the only kind of participation. I'm talking about parents helping their children become active participants in the learning process.'

'But, how can parents do that — they're not a part of what goes on in school.'

'I disagree. They *are* a part of what goes on in school — or an extension of it. Without them a school like this could never achieve its purpose — to teach kids how to learn. We don't have the resources to do it alone. That's why effective schools have to create a link between home and school.'

'But, how do you do that when parents lead busy lives — they're just too busy working to help teach their children to learn.'

'I'm not expecting that nor do I expect many parents could provide that kind of support. That's not the connection I'm talking about.'

'What is it?'

'It's a more subtle and more practical connection between home and school. It's the kind of connection with school that makes parents feel they, too, pass or fail depending on what happens to their child.'

'Don't all parents feel that way?'

'Not really, probably for a lot of reasons — such as both parents working, or the child comes from a single parent family, or a home with many siblings to care for, which may prevent the parent from having as close a relationship as they would like with their child. Today, there sometimes is a separation between home and school that can make the teacher's job more difficult than ever before.'

'Yes, I've written about what the average family is like today.'

'Well, every teacher needs to know what it's like in order to deal with it effectively. You can't ignore it or wish it away. It's here and it's affecting the life of practically every kid in the classroom.'

'But, what can any teacher do about it? These things are out of reach of the teacher.'

'That's an attitude that will get you in trouble in this school. The classroom is never far removed from all the problems that exist in the family and in the community. The classroom is the meeting ground where family, school and community come together. We can't expect learners to shed the powerful influence of family and community just because they walk into a place called "school".'

'But, what can a teacher do about it?'

'In one sense — home and family problems can't be the focus of schools. Teachers can't teach and be parents too, although some kids need both. I don't expect that and, frankly, teachers aren't paid to do both. But, there is another type of focus that is not only possible but necessary if a school is to be effective.'

'What's that?'

'In order to get kids attention — I mean actively engage them in the process of learning, the classroom has to be connected to the world in which they spend most of their time. Some say the emotional and physical maturity of kids today is years ahead of where it was fifty years ago. That makes even the early elementary student ready for real world problems and decision-making.'

'I never thought of it that way. But, I still don't see how a teacher can do anything about it.'

'It's by having an understanding that, while schools can't solve all of the problems learners come to school with, it can recognize them and take them into account in the classroom.'

'You mean like finding that a kid doesn't like to learn and changing what you teach to make school more interesting?'

'That's not what I mean. If you go too far with that attitude, you change the nature of school itself. Maybe your classroom becomes more like a recreational facility, a playground, or a penitentiary — that may keep learners interested or under control, but it won't help them learn. Remember, an effective school has direction and that direction has to get the learner to the next rung of the learning ladder. Give up on the ladder and you have your learners warming up for the big game but never getting to play. A lot of classrooms today have kids endlessly "warming up" with tasks that don't fit on the learning ladder.'

'You mean like having kids do busy work?'

'I mean like failing to ask students to solve problems and make decisions on their own with what they've learned. That's more serious and harder to spot.'

'OK, suppose I agree, but I don't see how the teacher can make the connection between home and school.'

'The type of family-school connection I'm talking about is called *communication*—communication between teacher and parent.'

'You mean notes and phone calls home.'

'That's a part of it but that's not the whole idea because, first of all, those devices are only used when a student's in trouble and, second, they're used so inconsistently that they really don't have the power to elicit parent support for the goals of the school and your classroom *over the entire school year*. Schools have to be where parents want to be as well as their kids.'

'You mean get them to participate in some way.'

'That's getting closer to the problem. The problem is that a school can no more be effective when teachers are excluded from participating in the decisions about it than when parents are excluded. And, today most parents *are* excluded.'

'But, like the problem with teachers, how do you do that?'

'The same.'

'What do you mean?'

'I mean this school is not my school and it's not the superintendent's school, although we are both ultimately responsible for it. This school is the teacher's school and the parent's school.'

'I know how you encouraged the participation of teachers in the decision-making of the school by making teachers responsible for solving problems in a lot of different areas, but I don't see how that can work with parents.'

'Well, just like teachers, what if every parent were asked to join or assigned to a team of other parents and teachers that was responsible for solving a school problem of concern *to parents*, for example, what to do to decrease our dropout rate, how to meet the needs of our gifted and talented, or increase the level of aspirations of our most disadvantaged students.'

'But, do parents really want to get that involved?'

'Not all and maybe not even most. But, an interesting thing happens when parents working with teachers on a problem that's relevant to them actually know that what they decide can and will be put into practice.'

'What's that?'

'They become interested in sharing the power *and the responsibility*. Even parents who never meet with their team or share their opinions get drawn into the decision-making process by receiving a newsletter from the team to which they were assigned or volunteered. In other words, they like being kept informed about the decisions being made by their group even when they can't actively participate.'

'Is that what you meant earlier when you said this characteristic of an effective school was *communication*?'

'That's it. Communication between parents and the school, even when it's not required or asked for by the parent. And, for those who choose to actively participate in the decision-making process — the results can be remarkable. The only way I can describe it is that a piece of the ownership of the school is transferred from me back to the community. Then, we truly have a *community school* — not because somebody said so or because teachers write notes home to parents but because the parents themselves have some of the power to make decisions that affect this school — big, important decisions that can influence the lives of their children for a long time to come.'

'Now I see how I came to talk with you in the first place. This school has a reputation for getting parents involved, and you've told me how this can be done. But, I have to ask, why aren't all schools doing this?'

'Many are, while others are in the process of discovering the importance of the family-school connection for themselves.'

'I'm beginning to see how schools need more than teachers, administrators and a curriculum to be effective — they need parents. But, I have another question that's been bothering me.'

'What's that?'

'How are the teachers in this school any different from other schools?'

'You'll need to ask my teachers that question. This school is not effective because of what I do; it's because of what my teachers do. Why not choose some teachers from this roster and ask *them*.' [*The principal reaches for a roster on her desk and hands it to her.*]

'Which ones should I talk with?'

'Any of them.'

'Wouldn't some be better than others?'

'You mean are some better teachers than others? Not in my opinion.'

'I'll let you make the choices. When you're finished, come back and tell me what you've learned.'

Reflections

1 Provide some recent evidence from your own experience that suggests that the classroom is never far removed from problems that exist in the family and in the community.

2 What would be an alternative to changing the curriculum for making school more interesting to your students? When might changing or modifying the curriculum be an appropriate strategy?

3 Describe some techniques you would use to initiate teacher-family communication that would make parents feel that they, too, pass or fail depending on what happens to their child.

4 What would you say to the response that not all, and maybe not even most, parents really want to get involved in school? What would be your approach for changing that attitude?

Field Activity

In the boxes below indicate the characteristics of three communities, one inner city, one suburban and one rural, that may indicate a difference in the availability of parents to become participants in their school. How might strategies to involve parents differ across these communities?

Community A (inner city):

Community B (suburban):

Community C (rural):

Effective Schools: Annotated
Readings

CONLEY, S. (1991) 'Review of research on teacher participation in school decision-making', *Review of Research in Education*, **17**, pp. 225–66.

This article reviews current research and practice on teacher participation in school decision-making. The author identifies the aims of teacher participation, the expectations teachers bring to the participation process and the areas of decision-making in which they can most effectively participate (dialogue 5).

CRUICKSHANK, D. (1990) *Research That Informs Teachers and Teacher Educators*, Bloomington, IN, Phi Delta Kappa.

This summary of research (1971–89) identifies the most studied and talked about characteristics of effective teachers and effective schools. The author provides a helpful summary table at the end that identifies forty-five characteristics of effectiveness pertaining to principals, teachers, and the classroom (dialogues 1–3).

Educational Leadership, May 1992, ASCD special issue on Using Performance Assessment, **49**, 8. Alexandria, VA.

This special issue contains examples of what teachers around the country are doing to give performance tests a try. Articles include illustrations of how performance tests are working in a variety of school settings and how they contribute to teacher and school effectiveness (dialogue 4).

Elementary School Journal, January 1991, Special issue on Educational Partnerships, **93**, 3. Chicago, IL, University of Chicago Press.

This special issue is devoted to how educators can establish educational partnerships between home, family and school.

The authors provide specific suggestions and describe practical programs which teachers and principals can use to improve family-school relations (dialogue 6).

GAZIEL, H. (1992) 'Team management patterns and school effectiveness,' *European Journal of Education*, **27**, 1/2, pp. 153–63.
This article examines the relationship between school effectiveness and school organization from the teacher's perspective. The structure of management teams and their decision-making patterns are studied to identify those characteristics that are most closely related to teacher satisfaction and school effectiveness (dialogue 5).

GRADY, M., WAYSON, W. and ZINKEL, P. (1989) *A Review of Effective Schools Research as it Relates to Effective Principals*, University Council for Educational Administration, 116 Farmer Bldg, Tempe, AZ.
This article reviews research that demonstrates the important relationship between effective schools and effective principals. The authors provide specific recommendations for how teachers can work together with principals to make their schools more effective (dialogues 2, 3 and 4).

MITCHELL, R. (1992) *Testing for Learning: How New Approaches to Evaluation Can Improve American Schools*, New York, The Free Press.
This book describes alternative approaches to traditional types of tests. The author discusses the problems of current standardized and norm-referenced testing practices, presents the advantages of assessing learner progress with performance tests, and provides many useful examples of 'authentic' assessments in the classroom (dialogue 4).

SMYLIE, M. (1992) 'Teacher participation in school decision making: Assessing willingness to participate', *Educational Evaluation and Policy Analysis*, spring, **14**, 1, pp. 53–67.
The author describes an original research study that identifies the organizational and psychological barriers to teacher participation and team decision-making. The findings reveal the important role of the principal for why and how teachers choose to participate in school decision-making (dialogue 5).

Part II:

What is an Effective Teacher?

7   The Power of Purpose

She scanned the roster for clues as to whom to visit. She circled the first name on the list, 'Mrs. Beecham', and called for an appointment. Mrs. Beecham agreed to meet with her on Tuesday at the end of her fifth period science class.

'Thank you for seeing me. As I mentioned on the phone, I'm writing a story about effective schools and effective teachers and I'd like to find out if the teachers in this school are any different than other teachers. I thought by talking to someone, like yourself, I could find out what it means to be an effective teacher.'

'Well, I think there are a lot of things that make a teacher effective. But, I'm afraid they aren't necessarily the kinds of things you can always see by coming into a classroom and observing for a few hours or even a day. For example, some — and maybe the most important — things that make a teacher effective have a lot to do with how you think about your job.'

'What do you mean?'

'I mean the demands of the job aren't always going to equal the rewards you're going to get — at least not the tangible ones. Teaching is a job that if you let it, can take more out of you than gets put back in.'

'I would think working hard and not being adequately rewarded would make you less effective.'

'But, I don't let it, because I balance the equation in other ways — get something back even more than what I put in. It's what every teacher who wants to be effective has to do.'

'But how do you do that — get more back then you put in?'

'By discovering a *purpose* for teaching that goes beyond just doing your job.'

'But how?'

'It starts with why you became a teacher in the first place — finding or, if necessary, rediscovering your own special reason for being in the classroom.'

'Don't most teachers know why they're teaching?'

'One of the greatest confusions that exists among beginning teachers is why they are teaching or even want to teach. Much of the time they're studying to become a teacher they're asking themselves — why? If they have entered the student teaching phase of their training, they know the job is tough, the working conditions difficult, and relative to other occupations of equal responsibility the pay is low.'

'So, why do they sacrifice so much for a job in which the rewards — at least the tangible ones — are low?'

'Well, if you ask them you'll hear some of them say that they want to be a teacher because they

> Feel a calling to help young children, *or*
> Like a particular subject or grade, *or*
> Want a career that assures them a job, *or*
> A job that allows time to raise a family.'

'Are these the purposes you were talking about?'

'You may find it surprising but none of these are sufficient to keep you in the teaching profession, once the reality of the job is experienced first hand. Good intentions for helping the young, love of second graders, summers off, and easy access to employment don't last very long when the demands of the task are truly understood. For some, this may take no longer than student teaching, after which more than a third never enter a classroom.'

'So, what are the kind of purposes that keep *you* teaching?'

'The kind of purposes I'm talking about and that any beginning teacher must find begins with a personal statement of what it is about teaching that you believe in. I've found that discovering your own purpose for teaching is difficult, since most of the purposes I've heard or read about are nothing more than vague and undifferentiated cliches that anyone could believe in.'

'Such as . . . ?'

'The things we've all heard so many times before. Such as:

> *Impart knowledge,*
> *Create growth and learning,*

> *Maximize student potential,*
> *Enhance student understanding,*
> *Foster self-esteem.'*

'I'm not sure I see the problem. Doesn't every teacher want to do these things?'

'I believe they do. That's not the problem. These words neither spark the personal meaning that motivates most teachers nor do they provide a personal feeling of accomplishment at the end of the day, since you rarely get to *see* them and they're influenced by many things outside your classroom.'

'So, what are good purposes?'

'Good purposes are specific and personally meaningful. They represent your own bedrock convictions — things you'd never compromise. They are deep abiding convictions that may have been buried within you for most of your adult life without you knowing it. They affect why you value some things and not others without even being conscious of their influence. They don't use cliches like "maximize potential" and fluffy words like "enhance" and "foster".'

'Could you give some examples?'

'They're personal to each individual.'

'Such as . . . ?'

'Well, if you grew up in a neighborhood where you felt racial or ethnic prejudice you might have a special understanding of its effects and how to overcome them. Or, if you're concerned about the rapid pace of science and technology, you might have a deep respect for the dangers as well as potential of science. Or, if your parents or grandparents came from another country or closely identify with another culture, you may have a special understanding of how other forms of government and customs can broaden an understanding of our own culture. Or, if you came from a family that encouraged a strong sense of cooperation and sharing, you may now be realizing the benefits of these characteristics in your own life. These are the types of things that may have been buried within you for a long time without you knowing it — yet they are an important part of you — a part that shouldn't be hidden in your classroom.

'I think I see how a purpose is something that's personally

meaningful, but I don't see how it can affect what you do in the classroom.'

'It won't unless your purpose is made to come 'alive' by influencing what you do and how you teach.'

'You mean by changing what you teach?'

'No, by influencing *how* you teach. For example, they might influence you:

> To discuss during social studies the effects of prejudice and how to overcome it, *or*
>
> To balance in a science class a respect for the potential as well as danger of science, *or*
>
> To explore in a history lesson how governments can limit human rights as well as create opportunities for them, *or*
>
> To teach during reading that each of us at times must take the responsibility for sharing our thoughts and feelings with others.'

'You're saying purposes are relevant to your own personal experiences?'

'Yes, and the experience of others you feel close to. You can bet that something unique has gone on in the lives of those who have them that make them even care about some things more than others.'

'But, for some purposes you'd have to change what you're teaching, wouldn't you?'

'Not the kind of purposes we're talking about. That's why purposes don't change the content you're teaching but the spirit and motivation for *how* you teach. They are ways in which you express *through the curriculum* who you really are — the things you believe in — that can make your teaching and your classroom special. No curriculum guide could dictate personal statements of purpose, yet each would fit into any curriculum guide. They are not lists of objectives. They are not even a guide to what you will teach on any given day. They're just one more reason to get up in the morning and want to come to your classroom. Although they may not motivate you every day of the school year, they bring a personal, silent touch to your classroom that reminds you why you are there.'

'How can a new teacher discover his or her purpose for teaching?'

'Your own purpose for teaching is discovered only after considerable soul-searching that turns up those special values in which you most deeply believe. They are not only nice things that people somewhere expect teachers to do but what *you* must do if you are to have pride in your work. Things you care about, remember as important from your own childhood experiences, learned from your family, experienced or failed to experience in your adult life and that you believe should be shared with others, serve as excellent personal statements of purpose.'

'Hmm, maybe I should find some of my own purposes for being a journalist?'

'We all have them, if we look for them. Think about yourself — who you really are, what you truly believe in and what you want to stand for — and, then, write down what you find. I think you'll be surprised that what you find was there all the time waiting to be discovered to remind you why you've chosen to become a journalist — and to motivate you to become a good one.

She thanked Mrs. Beecham, but left bewildered. She wondered what some of her own personal statements of purpose might be or if she really had any. She recalled the examples Mrs. Beecham had given, but had trouble thinking of her own unique purposes — purposes that could express who she was and what she believed in. She thought about her own bedrock convictions — what she really believed, would fight tooth and nail for and never give up. Thoughts rushed to her head that she had heard elsewhere and for a moment she was convinced that these were what she believed, too. But, then, she realized that the reason these thoughts had come to her so easily was that she had heard them many times before — from others who themselves were only repeating cliches they had heard many times before. It was as though she was being brainwashed to believe in somethings that were so good and beautiful that no one could deny their truth.

So, she thought longer and harder until she discovered she had been thinking too hard. The purposes she was seeking were all around her, in her room where she slept, in the clothes she wore, the friends she chose to be with, and how she spent her time. They were everywhere in the decisions she had made in life that expressed who she was — what she believed in, respected, admired, and wanted to become. In looking about she discovered that her entire life was a product of the decisions she had made that represented her values without ever having said to herself what those values were. She found, for example, that she

- *believed in personal **fitness and exercise**;*
- *liked to **analyze why** people act as they do;*
- *could tell successful people from unsuccessful people by **how organized** they were;*
- *believed the **longer you work** at something the more you'll like it;*
- *believed you only get to keep in life what you **give away**;*
- *believed anyone is free to do whatever they like — as long as they are willing to **face the consequences**;*
- *believed no one is **any stronger or weaker** than anyone else;*
- *believed the most important things in life we must **do ourselves**;*
- *liked people who weren't afraid to **share their feelings**.*

These, she felt, were beginning to express what Mrs. Beecham had been talking about — they were there all the time waiting to be discovered and brought to life as personal statements of purpose. Although she would have to think more about them, she knew these purposes were very much a part of her.

Reflections

1   What was Mrs. Beecham's solution to giving so much to a job in which the tangible rewards may be less than other jobs of equal responsibility?

2   Identify five commonly heard reasons for wanting to teach that Mrs. Beecham would *not* consider adequate to keep someone in the teaching profession.

3   With examples of your own, contrast 'good purposes' that are specific and personally meaningful with 'poor purposes' that are vague and undifferentiated cliches.

4   Construct your own list of purposes and share one of them with a classmate or with the class. Indicate when you first noticed its importance in your life. Give an example how it could be made to 'come alive' in your classroom.

Field Activity

From your own list of purposes, indicate in the box below how four of them could be implemented in your classroom. Indicate the grade, class or subject to which each of your purposes would apply.

1

2

3

4

8   The Balance Between Thinking and Performing

She called the next teacher on her list, Ms. Davis, who taught math and coached the girls' volleyball team. Ms. Davis consented to meet with her in the gym before practice the following Tuesday.

'Thank you for seeing me. I was talking with Mrs. Beecham, and she was saying how important it was that teachers have a purpose for teaching that expresses who they are — a reason for being in the classroom that provides its own personal reward. Is there anything else that makes an effective teacher?'

'One of the most important is to be aware of your own behavior.'

'You mean, know if what you're doing is right or wrong?'

'Not really. "Right" and "wrong" are words that *describe* your behavior, but they are not very useful in helping you *improve* your behavior.'

'Then, I'm not sure I know what you mean.'

'Good teaching isn't keeping a scorecard of "rights" and "wrongs". Every teacher makes mistakes — I mean errors of judgment like choosing to have a group discussion at the wrong time, or using an instructional technique that doesn't work, or giving an assignment that turns out to be over the kids' heads. Classrooms are filled with the unexpected — including the classrooms of experienced teachers. It's just their nature — life in classrooms is just too complicated to always predict what will and won't work. So, there'll be plenty of times things will go wrong.'

'But what about the times things go right. Shouldn't every teacher be aware of them?'

'Of course, but wanting and planning for success is different than chasing after it. Once your world revolves around a scorecard of what goes right and wrong in your classroom, you lose your natural instincts as a teacher — your decision-making

becomes less flexible hoping to improve the score in your favor
— and the more you try, the less natural you become. That's the
time you should be concentrating on your own behavior — not
what *someone else* might think of your behavior.'

'But, isn't what someone else thinks important?'

'Not at the time you're teaching. If you're worrying about
success or failure, you'll start searching for what you think others
would expect or want you to do and you'll be less aware of your
own behavior.'

'I think I've had that feeling.'

'We've all had it — particularly when we're new at something or are trying something out for the first time. Because we
lack confidence, we're always worrying about what someone else
will think.'

'Why is that?'

'Because I believe there are two very strong and often contra-
dictory parts of us. One part likes to take control of our behavior.
I call it *Self 1*. That part of us says, "Do what I say and when it's
all over I'll let you know how good you were."'

'That sounds like pretty important information for improving ourselves.'

'It would be, except that there's another side to us.'

'What's that?'

'It's the part of us that actually follows the commands of
Self 1 and does all the work — our *Self 2*, you might say.'

'How do these two sides of us affect how to teach?'

'I can sometimes see them working when I observe a student teacher. They're confronted with an unexpected decision.
So, Self 1 goes to work rapidly searching through years of formal
schooling and experience with similar problems. When it finds
the best match between a previously learned response and what's
happening to them at the moment, it gives the command to Self
2 for execution. The result is not a bad response but neither is it
a response having the grace and balance for which that individual
is capable — and, in fact, had shown before when the situation
was less demanding or tense.'

'And why was that?'

'Because along with Self 1 came self-doubts about whether
what was chosen would be right or wrong.'

'You mean they started to worry about their success or failure again?'

'That's right. We all have the tendency to judge ourselves at the very moment we are making an important decision — which unknown to us breaks our concentration and makes our decision less genuine and natural. Instinctively, we do what we think others would want us to do — not what our feelings and the events before us are telling us to do.'

'And is that because we're worried about not making a mistake?'

'Yes — thanks to the critical self-judgment of Self 1.'

'But what if, as you say, you're capable of a better response . . . ?'

'There's another alternative. The teacher can become aware of the distracting influence of Self 1, and shut down its influence on Self 2. What happens next is that a conscious decision is made to change from a *thinking self* to a *feeling self*. In other words, the teacher stops looking for the right thing to say or do, and responds, you might say, from the heart.'

'And, then, what happens?'

'What happens at that point is what star athletes and performers do instinctively. They use their Self 1 to learn the rules of the game or their musical notes, but once learned they listen to their performing self, Self 2.'

'Is that because things are moving so fast, they don't have time to think or to remember?'

'That's right. Just like in a hectic fast-paced classroom — there's not time to consult their thinking self. They have to rely on their feelings which have been influenced by previous schooling and experience but are no longer completely determined by it. If they are truly successful performers — or effective teachers — the effects of Self 1 have been absorbed into a kind of *feeling sense* that directs their actions and is in command of the show. That's how some teachers give the performance of their life while others are worrying about the right thing to say or do.'

'But, I still don't see what anyone can do about the critical judgments being passed along by Self 1.'

'Well, some teachers don't do anything about it and that's the problem. You see, they're always worried about their success or failure — always judging themselves by past experience or what others might think to the point that their natural instincts are stifled by their own self-doubts. Then, they're no longer capable of feeling what the best response is. They can only choose a response from among those they have already learned.'

'And, you're saying that maybe there's none there that really fits?'

'That's right; many times there isn't. Classrooms are too complex — create too many unanticipated events that are just different enough from the one before to knock the props out of any decision-making strategy that relies solely on previously acquired responses.'

'So, what does a teacher do?'

'With experience they learn a different approach.'

'Which is . . . ?'

'They learn to subdue the critical judgments of Self 1 and create a new response which may never have occurred before.'

'How?'

'By becoming vigilant observers of their own actions without passing judgment on them.'

'Isn't that difficult?'

'Do you know the difference between a good coach and a poor one?'

'I'm afraid not.'

'The good coach helps you associate your actions with your feelings, non-judgmentally. Their role is to teach the player to be a good observer of his or her own behavior — to acquire a keen eye so that the player is always aware where the critical parts of the body are at what times. The coach, at least a good one, doesn't shout "No, that's wrong!", but rather says, "Look where your arm is. Is that where you want it to be?" See the difference.'

'I'm not sure.'

'In the first instance the player may not know how to solve the problem, since he or she will be wondering how high the coach wants him to place her arm. In the second, the coach is asking the player to first become *aware of her own behavior* and, then, to think about where it should be. Where it should be might be where the coach told her, a textbook illustrated, or she scored her last point. It's where things feel comfortable and natural. Notice, nothing positive or negative was said. Instead, the player was led to become an observer of those parts of the environment most relevant to the performance being required and to search for and become conscious of what happened. In teaching as well as in coaching — non-judgmental observation is indispensable for the unbroken concentration needed for your best performance.'

'That was an interesting description of what may happen on a volleyball court or playing field. But, is it really what effective teachers do in the classroom?'

'I think it is. They create new responses from their own feelings, as opposed to selecting responses that were previously learned. In the latter case, they're trying to make happen the consequences that they've been taught should follow from their actions. In the former, they're doing what is required by the conditions before them — albeit influenced by acquired knowledge and experience.'

'And because of the unpredictability of events in the classroom, those consequences you've learned to expect don't always occur. Now I see — if you expect them and they don't occur — you think you've failed.'

'Exactly. And with that strategy a teacher is bound to fail more than succeed, since consequences learned at an earlier time don't often repeat themselves in today's classrooms. To stay in that stage for very long will create more and more self-doubts which makes your ability to be non judgmental about your own behavior nearly impossible.'

'Can teachers get beyond that stage?'

'It's the only way a teacher can keep up with the fast pace of events in the classroom. They have to be aware of their own behavior enough to develop a sense of what feels comfortable and appropriate — they have to develop their *feeling sense*. Teachers who develop a feeling sense don't worry about success or failure; they focus on becoming aware of their own behavior.'

'And are you saying any teacher can do this?'

'Yes, if they're willing to set aside some old mental habits and acquire some new ones.'

'You mean be aware of their own behavior without being judgmental?'

'Yes, then they can become more conscious of their behavior and their feelings about it — that's what develops their feeling sense.'

'I'm afraid I've never heard about this *feeling sense* before. Would you mind if I talked with some of the other teachers about it?'

'Not at all. Mr. Koker might be someone you'd enjoy talking with.'

'I'll try to see him next.'

Reflections

1 From your own experience, describe a personal incident in which you were worried about saying or doing the 'right' thing. How aware of your own behavior were you at the moment?

2 How would you describe *Self 1* and *Self 2* in a way that would be recognizable to

 • a professional football player
 • a rush hour busdriver
 • a neurosurgeon
 • a junior high teacher

3 Mrs. Beecham suggested some ways in which we could heighten our ability to become non-judgmental observers of our behavior. What were her suggestions?

4 What role does previously acquired knowledge and experience play in the development of our *feeling sense*?

5 Consider the following dialogue:

Teacher: Now I want you to finish the problems on page 70 before the end of class.
Mark: (shouting out) I'm not gonna do anymore of these dumb problems.
Teacher: You know the rules, Mark . . . obey your teacher.
Mark: The rules are stupid!
Teacher: That's not the way we're supposed to behave in class, Mark.
Mark: (quietly, but so the teacher could hear) . . . that's tuff.
Teacher: If you don't get to work, you'll get ten more for homework and a visit to the principal's office.

Create an alternative dialogue that illustrates a teacher who uses her feeling sense to depart from the above script.

Field Activity

Indicate in the box below four specific instances in which a teacher you've observed departed from an expected routine to respond with their *feeling sense*. What was the effect on the learner?

1

2

3

4

9   Discovering Flow

She thought about the things Mrs. Davis had said. Like her discovery of an effective school, much of what she was hearing was not what she expected. She had hoped to hear about the strategies and techniques of effective teachers — how they use attention-gaining devices to motivate learners, advance organizers to introduce new content, behavioral objectives to focus on important outcomes, and unit and lesson plans to organize the curriculum. But, instead, she heard of purposes that express who you are, Self 1 and 2, and the feeling sense. These were things about teaching she had not heard before and wanted to know more about. For her next appointment, she called on Mr. Koker, a tenth year social studies teacher, who consented to meet with her during his planning period on Monday. She was determined to continue her questioning to uncover all there was to know about being an effective teacher.

'Thank you for seeing me, Mr. Koker. Ms. Davis was telling me how important it was to view your teaching non-judgmentally — like a detached umpire or coach.'

'Well, I think she's trying to tell you something that every new teacher has to go through.'

'What's that?'

'That we come to the classroom with a lot of self-doubts about our own abilities. And, then, we discover how much these self-doubts consume our decision-making — worrying about this and that until we no longer are in touch with our natural instincts.'

'Yes, I think that was it.'

'It's what every new teacher faces until you discover *flow*.'

'What's *that*?'

Flow is linking your feelings with what's happening at the moment. You see, with the fast pace of events in classrooms, you can't always match up previous solutions with what's happening

Becoming a Teacher

and, so, you have to have flow to link the two in a more flexible and spontaneous way.

'I'm not sure I understand.'

'What I'm saying is that flow is a way of creating original responses to unanticipated events. When you have flow, what you've learned in the past isn't just transferred to the present — it's changed to fit the learners in front of you who have their own unique interests, learning histories, and abilities.'

'Every teacher must try to use what they've learned from school or previous experience in their classroom. What's wrong with that?'

'It's the secure thing to do and most new teachers do it. But, the problem is that the conditions before you may not be like anything you've experienced in the past. What I'm trying to describe is how rapid and spontaneous decision-making has to be in the classroom. I must make a hundred decisions — real decisions — every day that effect the lives of my students.'

'Why so many?'

'Because everything is always moving — changing to present a new set of conditions. In other words, classrooms are unpredictable. Your mailman would go crazy if each day he or she had to look in a different place for the mailbox, as would the head of a company if each day the company changed the business it were in, or a surgeon if he or she had to operate on aliens from outer space whose internal organs kept changing depending on what planet they were from.'

'Are you saying that's the kind of variety a teacher faces?'

'Yes, many of us face just such variety for which no amount of training outside the classroom can adequately prepare you.'

'So what does a teacher do?'

'Meet variety with variety.'

'You mean create new responses with flow?'

'Yes. For each unexpected event — and there are hundreds each day — there must be an equally unique response that matches it in intensity and variety. For those teachers who have not learned to create, innovate, and change their behavior in response to what's happening around them, the variety they will face will be far greater than that which they can provide.'

'And, then, what?'

'They lose control of their own behavior — always *reacting* to the behavior of others because they can't *create* a new response or change an old one to better fit the occasion. They can't change the script they've learned at some earlier time or the 'program' they've become accustomed to.'

'So, what stops new teachers from changing the script or program?'

'Their own self-imposed fears.'

'Such as . . . ?'

'They take many forms, but for new teachers they can include fears like:

- Calling on the real bright kids
- Changing the order of things in the text
- Having kids work in groups
- Stopping in the middle of a lesson to review
- Being seen as too "soft" — or too "cold"
- Skipping what doesn't work
- Giving too many high grades — or low grades
- Substituting materials at a different level
- Talking about their problems with more experienced teachers

'These kinds of fears are the imaginary walls to creative and innovative responses. They are barriers that prevent the new teacher from changing.'

'Don't experienced teachers have fears, too — maybe different kinds — but fears just the same?'

'Probably so, but if they are to be effective they don't let them get in their way. They've stopped judging themselves and so they can make mistakes without self-recrimination.'

'They make mistakes too?'

'Well, that's an interesting point. I've been a teacher for ten years and I can say that both experienced and beginning teachers make many mistakes, for example, how to handle a behavior problem, select the proper level for an assignment, go at a certain pace, or when to test and when to review.'

'That's difficult for me to believe.'

'I know what you're thinking — that effective teachers don't make mistakes. But, frankly, mistakes — errors of judgment — are inevitable in large numbers in *any* classroom.'

'I guess what you're saying is that like in sports even the best team gets scored on?'

'And, some good teams get scored on quiet a bit.'

'So, then, what separates effective and less effective teachers if it's not errors of judgment — which, as you say, are going to happen in every classroom?'

'It's the extent to which effective teachers allow themselves to become aware of their mistakes and change the conditions under which they are most likely to occur.'

'Mrs. Davis would say they acquire a kind of feeling sense. And, you're saying that when it's wrong the teacher will be aware of it.'

'You bet, if they've stopped being critical of their own behavior long enough to experience it themselves.'

'But, how?'

'By not worrying about the expected consequences of their actions and by being aware of their own behavior. Then, you can see and remember what you did — and what to change. Most new teachers have little conscious recollection of their behavior in the classroom and don't know what they did to make things right or wrong. They were too busy worrying about whether the consequences they were expecting would occur.'

'I guess that's what Mrs. Davis was talking about when she said you have to rely on your *feeling sense* to tell you what works and what doesn't.'

'I think she's right. It's connecting up your own behavior — what you've just done — with a kind of feeling that tells you how comfortable you are with it. That's really what effective teaching is all about — acquiring a sense of what will work and what won't without having to look it up in some textbook or remember what you've done before.'

'But, somewhere you have to relate the decisions you make with their consequences on the learner, don't you? I'm thinking of a teacher listening to his or her feelings but having a lousy impact on kids. That's a real possibility, isn't it?'

'It is. But, classrooms are too unpredictable — influenced by too many things to draw judgments about one's behavior from *only* expected consequences. But, I do agree with you that consequences are important, since it's what schools are all about. Kids need to learn and to grow and while the teacher may not be the only influence on learning, she or he is one of the most important.'

'That was my point. So, where do consequences — learning and growth — come in?'

'Well, first I think it would be a mistake to believe that effective teachers aren't interested in consequences. They are and very much so. In fact, I believe it's one of the characteristics that separates experienced and inexperienced teachers the most.'

'Where do they come in, then?'

'Perhaps not in the way you think.'

'Then, how?'

Every decision that a teacher makes is influenced by a desired consequence. So, even before a teacher forms a response — decides what to do — a consequence has been imagined — the teacher wants Johnny to stop talking, Alex to get the math problem correct, or Amanda to repeat the steps needed to answer the question. Then, of course, the teacher wants to see if what was done to teach them to do these things actually worked. And, there again consequences creep back in. So consequences are — or at least should be — at the beginning and end of every decision that's made.'

'Then, I don't understand why someone wouldn't be fearful of the consequence — afraid that what they had hoped for didn't happen?'

'But, fear isn't something you have *after* an outcome has already occurred — it's something you have in *anticipation* of an outcome. After the outcome has occurred you might be disappointed that what you've tried didn't work but you really wouldn't be experiencing fear. It's not the consequences that *have occurred* that you're fearful of — it's the *expected* consequences you've been anticipating and that might not occur that prevents you from being aware of your own behavior.'

'You're saying that a focus on expected consequences isn't helpful *while* you're teaching because that's what produces the fear and the inability to change your behavior.'

'That's right, because I don't think artists, musicians, or

athletes worry much about consequences while in the process of performing — and, if they did, I bet they'd have a lousy performance.'

'But, that isn't saying they don't care about consequences.'

'That's right. They had consequences in mind before they began the performance and again when they were finished — when they listened to the applause, counted the number in the audience, or waited for the referee's decision. But, in between they could *change* their behavior — and often — to fit their *feeling sense*, because they were concentrating on their own behavior not the previously learned consequences they may have been expecting.'

'But, I don't see how a focus on consequences afterward, then, can be very useful — other than as a kind of personal reward or message of discouragement.'

'Well, you may not recognize it but knowledge of results develops your feeling sense and makes it more identifiable for the next performance. If it *is* what you wanted, your feeling sense gets stronger. If it's not what you wanted, your feeling sense gets weaker. But, you have to be aware of your own behavior at the time you are performing to make the connection between feelings and consequences.'

'You're talking like this feeling sense is a real thing — a kind of organ inside us.'

'Your feeling sense is always there inside of you whether you like it or not — you just become more aware of it when your mind isn't all cluttered up with anticipating certain consequences at the time you're performing. This is exactly what happens when someone acquires *flow* and becomes a professional at their job — an athlete who wins against a bigger opponent, a bus driver who negotiates rush hour traffic, a surgeon who deals with complications, a salesclerk who pleases a disgruntled patron, or a teacher who inspires a class of unmotivated and combatant learners. They have to be so in touch with their *feeling sense* that they can change their behavior to suit the conditions before them in ways that may not be like any behavior they've learned in the past. In other words, they can rewrite the script or program as many times as they need for an outstanding performance.'

'So, that's what flow is all about.'

'Now you know. It's not what some might think — that

flow requires big changes in instructional technique or strategy from outside the classroom. Real flow represents little changes that by virtue of their responsiveness to learners comes from teachers who have developed their feeling sense.'

Reflections

1   In your own words, describe what Mr. Koker means by *flow*. Give an example in your own life of how you have used flow to get through a difficult and unanticipated event.

2   Explain how we come to acquire fears in teaching and at what times they most frequently occur. What typically are their effects on our teaching behavior?

3   Make a list of your five greatest fears in being in the classroom. What would be some of the ways you might depart from the program or script that might reduce or eliminate each of these fears?

4   What is the relationship between flow and creativity? Provide an example of how you could achieve flow by being creative.

5   In the words of Mrs. Davis, list three characteristics that describe the feeling sense and in the words of Mr. Koker, three characteristics that describe flow. Are they describing the same thing?

Field Activity

Indicate in the box below four instances of creativity in the classroom that resulted from teachers who had *flow*.

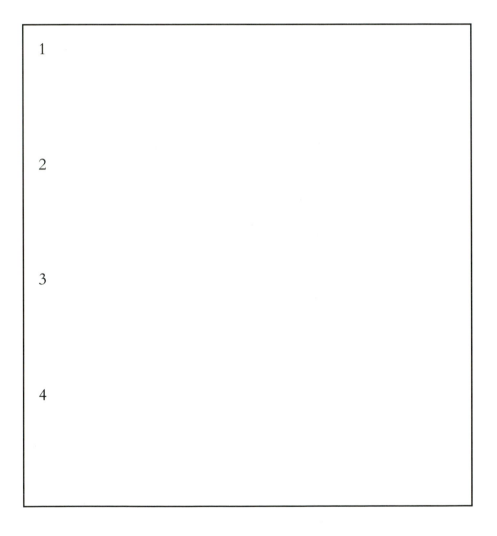

1

2

3

4

10 Stages of Growth

She decided to take time to summarize some of what she had learned from her visits thus far. Some things she felt she understood, but there were others that were unclear — like how one really acquires flow, learns to shut down the distracting influence of Self 1, and provide creative responses to the changing conditions of the classroom. These surely, she thought, were important questions that would need to be answered before she could write her story.

To try to recall what she had learned so far, she decided to jot down the most vivid impressions made by each of the teachers with whom she had talked. The task was not easy, since many of her discussions were about topics with which she had little familiarity. They were, she thought, perspectives — or ways of thinking — that could not be easily described in the conventional language of teaching. She even thought to herself that maybe that was why it was so difficult to be an effective teacher — one had to go beyond convention to acquire a perspective or attitude that could adapt the strategies and techniques of teaching to your own classroom.

Slowly, her list took shape. She jotted down each idea she could remember alongside the teacher from whom she had heard it.

Mrs. Beecham

- *Teachers should have their own unique purposes for teaching that express who they are.*
- *The best purposes for teaching are personally meaningful — representing your own bedrock convictions — things you believe in, would fight tooth and nail for and would never compromise.*

- *Statements of purpose are your own personal reasons for why teaching and your classroom is special to you.*
- *Be careful of 'nice' purposes or 'wonderful' purposes — they may not be **your** purposes.*

Ms. Davis

- *'Right' and 'wrong' are words that describe our behavior but which may not be helpful in improving it.*
- *There are two sides to our behavior that direct our decision-making — Self 1 that tells us what to do and critically judges how well we do it, and Self 2 that performs the action.*
- *When we observe our own behavior without expecting previously learned consequences, we limit the critical self-judgment of Self 1 and allow Self 2 to perform, making our responses quicker and more natural to unanticipated events.*
- *Effective teachers rely on a feeling sense which is influenced by their previous schooling and experience but not completely determined by it.*
- *You develop your feeling sense by becoming aware of your behavior and your own comfort with it at the time you are performing.*

Mr. Koker

- *The unpredictability of events in classrooms seldom allows the consequences we expect to occur.*
- *Flow is linking your feeling sense with what's happening at the moment to create new responses to unanticipated events.*
- *Effective teaching requires a variety of responses for which no amount of preparation outside the classroom can adequately prepare you.*
- *Flow is being able to match the variety of student responses with a variety of teacher reactions, many of which may never have occurred before, thereby changing the script or 'program' you've become accustomed to.*

- *What distinguishes effective from less effective teachers is that effective teachers allow themselves to become aware of their own behavior and to learn from it. This is how they develop their feeling sense.*

Now she was ready to discuss some of these ideas with other teachers on her list. For her next appointment she chose Mrs. Thomas — a social studies teacher — who had been mentioned as one of the most experienced teachers in the school. Mrs. Thomas agreed to meet before her first class on Wednesday.

'Mrs. Thomas, as you know, I've been talking to some of the other teachers about what it means to be an effective teacher. And, quite frankly, the picture I'm getting is a lot different then I expected.'

'What do you mean?'

'Well, I expected to hear a lot about behavioral objectives, lesson plans, individualizing instruction — things like that — but, instead I find what I'm hearing is . . . well . . . a lot different, involving things like how you think about yourself as a teacher and your job, your values, and how you become aware of your own behavior and learn to create new responses. Now, I know you're one of the most experienced teachers in this school. So, I very much would like to get your opinion on some of the things I've been hearing.'

'Like what?'

'Well, for example, why new teachers are so concerned with what others may think of them and judge themselves so critically.'

'New teachers do have a lot of fears — fears like not being able to control the class, of whether the students really like them or not, and doing well when their principal may be watching. And, yes, these fears do limit their effectiveness. But, they are also a *natural* part of becoming an effective teacher.'

'They are!'

'The point is not that teachers, especially new teachers, have fears that limit their effectiveness but how quickly the new teacher moves to more mature stages of his or her development.'

'You mean there are actual stages that teachers go through in becoming effective?'

'I call them levels of concerns because with each stage there are new and different concerns which are the focus of attention.'

'What are they?'

'Well, the first is what you were just talking about. It's what I call a concern for *self-survival*. It's the first and most elementary stage of professional growth through which most teachers pass.'

'What's it like?'

'In this stage the teacher is almost exclusively concerned with his or her survival — getting through the day, looking good in the eyes of others, and controlling the class. Teachers at this stage are driven by their own anxieties and fears and a concern for appearance.'

'I would imagine a first-year teacher would feel terribly insecure.'

'Many are. And, of course, in the beginning there will be some disappointments, which can make matters worse.'

'This must be why Ms. Davis said that effective teachers don't divide things into "right" and "wrong," but concentrate on their own standard of comfort and appropriateness with what they're doing. They become aware of their behavior apart from the previously learned consequences that they might expect.'

'I think she was describing a teacher who had gone beyond a concern for his or her own survival. But, most teachers must live through this first stage until they get enough confidence not to judge their actions in terms of what they've learned to expect. It's where most of us are when we begin teaching.'

'Do teachers stay in this stage for very long?'

'Some stay in it longer than others. They are teachers who have a continual need for direction, often experience intense feelings of insecurity, and, to hide their own anxiety, sometimes take on a face-saving authoritarian style.'

'How do they teach?'

'By presenting things that are safe — that keeps the class under control — but not necessarily learning.'

'And, how do they get beyond this stage?'

'Most teachers reach it naturally simply because it's so

exhausting to stay survival-oriented for very long. In the next stage, teachers exchange a *self-orientation* for a *task-orientation*.'

'What does that mean?'

'They establish routines and become highly organized — sometimes so organized that they may have a good deal of trouble ever altering what they do.'

'You mean they never want to change?'

'That's right. They don't want to do anything that upsets the status quo — the nice predictable world they've so carefully organized for themselves. They sometimes spend more time and energy making themselves secure than teaching. They repeat their successes — what works for them, time and again.'

'Kind of like being on cruise control.'

'That's it — rigid in their patterns and resisting changing to new conditions.'

'But, I'm not sure I see the danger in being organized — isn't that something every teacher should be.'

'Except when your pattern of behavior is so organized that you never take the risks needed to change, to become responsive to the needs of your students, which are continually changing. These teachers are successful but only in covering the content in tried and true ways.'

'Now, there must be another stage.'

'There is. It represents the highest level of professional growth in which the teacher is *student-oriented*.'

'What does that mean?'

'It means their first and foremost concern is not with themselves or with the mechanics of teaching but with their students. They are consumed with an interest in and concern for the impact they are having on the lives of their students.'

'Do they have specific concerns like teachers at the other stages?'

'They have concerns such as how to challenge unmotivated students, what to do to assure that their students know how to apply what they are learning, and how well they are meeting the social and emotional needs of their students. In short, they are concerned with whether or not their students are growing and changing. And, because they are secure and free of anxieties about their own performance, they can take risks.'

'How do they do that?'

'They look for ways to fit ideas together in new and unusual ways. They take instructional resources others may have discarded or failed to notice and use them to create new and innovative solutions to problems.'

'Teachers at this stage of concern sound a lot like the teachers Mr. Koker was describing who have flow. They create new responses that match the needs of their students.'

'Yes, they are creative by integrating into their teaching new and sometimes untried behaviors, procedures or materials with an eye for their impact on student learning — expending their valuable but limited energy where it counts the most.'

'How does a teacher who is student-oriented differ from, say, one who is survival or task-oriented?'

'What you'd notice would be that these teachers are in touch with the interests and ability levels of their students. They search for innovative solutions, are highly adaptable and flexible, and are prone to take risks by suggesting new plans and ideas that take their learners to the next rung of the learning ladder.'

'Does every teacher have to go through the first two stages to arrive at the third? It seems an awfully time consuming way of becoming an effective teacher?'

'That's an interesting point. And, while I've seen many teachers go through each stage, I don't believe it's the best or only way of becoming an effective teacher.'

'You mean plodding through the initial levels of concern may not be necessary for attaining the third and highest level of concern?'

'This is what happens to some new teachers who "hit the classroom running". They have already arrived at a way of thinking and acting that emulates a concern for their impact on students.'

'So they don't need to spend time with their own fears for survival or a rigid organizational routine that may isolate them from being responsive to student needs.'

'That's right. Like the effective teacher of long standing, their primary concern is with their impact on students that enables them to deliver creative responses that fit their students unique learning needs.'

'Thanks. You've given me some more things to think about.'

Reflections

1   Recall our dialogues with Mrs. Beecham, Ms. Davis and Mr. Koker. If you had visited each of them, what would be the one thing you would remember most from each visit?

2   Describe some of the concerns that a teacher might have at each of the three stages of growth. What is the primary focus of a teacher's attention at each stage?

3   Do you believe a teacher has to go through the first and second stage of concern to reach the third? What might be some of the things a teacher could do to speed up the process — or skip a stage altogether?

4   At what stage of concern is a teacher most likely to acquire flow? How would you characterize a teacher's instructional style at this stage?

5   Assign the following teacher concerns to the stage of professional growth to which they most likely belong.

❑   Whether the students really like me
❑   Challenging unmotivated students
❑   How to use cooperative learning techniques
❑   Increasing students' feelings of accomplishment
❑   Doing well when I'm observed
❑   Learning how to use a computer to write lesson plans
❑   Whether students can apply what they know
❑   Losing the respect of my students
❑   Planning instructional routines

Field Activity

In the box below list six of *your* most prominent concerns as a beginning year teacher. Then, go back and classify each in terms of *self, task* and *student*. Which classification is most represented?

1

2

3

4

5

6

11 Culturally Diverse and Heterogeneous Classrooms

For her next appointment, she wanted to talk with a beginning teacher. She especially wanted to find out how a new teacher handled the culturally diverse and heterogeneous classes she was seeing all around her that might make the highest stage of professional growth, a concern for students, difficult to achieve. Mr. Randall, a second year English teacher, consented to meet with her at lunch.

'Thank you for seeing me, Mr. Randall. I wanted to hear what sort of challenge a new teacher, like yourself, faces in teaching in a school like this. If I read the future correctly, many of tomorrow's classrooms will represent large numbers of students with many of the diverse learning needs represented in this school.'

'I think you may be describing a lot of classrooms today.'

'And, so, I was wondering how you deal with it — or whether it makes a difference?'

'I think it makes a big difference.'

'What do you mean?'

'Well, for example, most of the instructional events included in a model lesson plan like: gaining attention, stating the objective, presenting content, obtaining a response — you know them — don't seem to work as well in a culturally diverse or heterogeneously grouped classroom of, say, thirty to thirty-five students as in a smaller more homogeneous classroom.'

'Why not?'

'While they're important, I've found that, by themselves, they're not enough to get students actively involved in the goals of your lesson.'

'Why not?'

'Because students in large heterogeneous classes — those with many different learning needs — are not ready to give up

some of their independence to someone to whom they are not yet fully committed. Their behavior is more independent and willful at the start of a lesson. In large heterogeneous classrooms, the structure of a classroom and the teacher's routine aren't sufficient to secure their commitment to learn, as it might be in a smaller more homogeneous class of learners.'

'So what do you do?'

'You recognize that the class perceives themselves as decision-makers.'

'And, how do you do that?'

'By establishing a *climate for decision-making*. The key to establishing a climate for decision-making is to create a classroom that encourages students to use their independence in ways that can achieve the goals of your classroom. In other words, your goals must become their goals without taking away the independence and willfulness they know they have.'

'And, how do you do that?'

'It begins by acknowledging your student's strengths. In other words, successful teachers of large heterogeneous classes begin by informing their students what they have *learned*, *accomplished* or *mastered*. While conveying weaknesses takes authority away from the learner, expressing strengths gives authority and recognition to the learner. Now, students more readily see themselves as decision-makers who can regulate and participate in their own learning. The tables are turned and the momentum of the classroom is working for not against you.'

'That's how you establish a decision-making climate?'

'You also have to make it happen.'

'How?'

'One way is with questions.'

'What kind of questions?'

'A type of question that is helpful in establishing a climate for decision-making is the *situation* question.'

'What's that?'

'Situation questions collect facts, information and background about your learners' understanding of a topic — before you begin to teach. They try and discover strengths but also to uncover concerns and anxieties that, later, can become impediments to learning. Situation questions introduce the topic and, because they voluntarily solicit information from the learner, they don't have to be evaluated as either right or wrong.

'What are some examples of situation questions?'

'Oh, for example,
What is one of *your* most common errors in punctuation?
Who knows what the word combustion means?
Can *anyone* tell us how the early inhabitants of North America
     got here?
What does the word democracy mean to *you*?'

'Situation questions attempt to explain through the students' own responses the value of the lesson in *their* language and from *their* point of view. When the students feel their ideas are part of your lesson, they're more likely to talk about the content and feel enthusiasm for it. The objective of a situation question is to open the lesson and to provide the necessary background for learning to begin.'

'And once you've established a decision-making climate with situation questions, then what?'

'You have to *establish a need*.'

'How do you do that?'

'Establishing a need involves finding out something about your learners that relates to the lesson. It means getting the learners to perceive the importance of what is about to be taught in terms of their, not the teacher's, world.'

'In smaller more homogeneous classrooms the learner equates personal need with teacher goals. If the teacher says it's important by virtue of making it the goal of the lesson — then, the student feels, "I must need it." But, learners in large heterogeneous classrooms rarely buy this reasoning.'

'You mean some students in large heterogeneous classrooms are unwilling to exchange their needs for what, to them, are the needs of the teacher?'

'That's right. It's tricky — substituting student needs for teacher needs.'

'It even sounds like letting students decide for themselves what should be taught.'

'It does. But, the aim is not to alter or reinterpret the curriculum solely according to student interests. It's the other way around — to illuminate student interests in such a way that makes the curriculum *relevant*. In other words, student perceptions about the curriculum are changed, not the curriculum.'

'Can the teacher really do that?'

'Yes, the teachers I know find that their curriculum can come "alive" without changing the curriculum or reinterpreting it in terms of lower expectations for their learners. The element that is sometimes missing in heterogeneous classrooms is *relevance*.'

'But, isn't relevance important in every classroom?'

'Of course, but in smaller, more homogeneous classes the structure of the classroom and the teacher's routine may be sufficient to secure a commitment to learn without special attention to making the content relevant. There, the curriculum materials, homogeneous values of the learners, and natural dialogue of the classroom may adequately convey the relevance of what is to be learned. In large heterogeneous classrooms the case for relevance must be made more explicitly *by the teacher*.'

'How do you create relevance?'

'This is the unique role of the teacher of heterogeneous classes. Their role is to create a context for instruction that makes the content and their students' ability to comprehend it relevant.'

'And, they do that by . . . ?'

'. . . by establishing a need in the context of a problem. For the successful teacher the bridge between learner and content is made by presenting content in the context of problems that relate to real or perceived student needs. Needs are to learners what objectives are to teachers.'

'You mean they're the same thing?'

'Opposite sides of the same coin, you might say. Each represents the common theme of a lesson from different perspectives.'

'But how do you establish a need that your students may not know they have?'

'In large heterogeneous classrooms needs can be established by posing *problem* questions. Problems create needs. And, where there are needs, there is a context for learning that supports student independence and willfulness in a decision-making context.'

'I'm not sure what a problem question is.'

'Problem questions raise difficulties and contradictions that point to a need that may not be obvious to your students. They illuminate contradictions or irregularities that call for the creation of a solution, a will to act or to change a way of doing things. Problems and the contradictions they bring to light are inherently interesting to students. "Trouble" is what learners like, since their own world is so often marked by it. Problem questions spell out the trouble in a particular situation or context.'

'What are some examples of problem questions?'

'Well, for example,

> *If* someone were to see written "Mr. Burns nurse," *how* would the reader know whether the man's name is Burn or Burns?
>
> *If* someone were to mix air, fire and gasoline together to produce power, *how* might its destructive forces be controlled?
>
> *How* did the North American continent become inhabited *if*, as many scientists believe, our civilization actually began in a place near what is now known as Egypt?
>
> *If* democracy means freedom, then *why* are we not free to do as we please in our own democracy?

Each of these questions state a problem — but not just any problem. They are problems that present a contradiction or irregularity that raises the excitement of learning by accentuating a dilemma that your students can resolve within your classroom and the goals of your lesson.'

'Are there any other types of questions I should know about?'

'In large heterogeneous classrooms the teacher must also *demonstrate capability*. In these classrooms respect and the attention that follows is not easily won. The mere presence of the teacher behind the desk, or at the chalkboard doesn't guarantee sufficient commitment from students for learning to occur.'

'Why not?'

'One reason is that some teachers in these classrooms confuse presenting content — delivering the lesson — with demonstrating capability. The former requires the teacher to present the content and activities of a lesson *as dictated by* the curriculum, while the latter requires the teacher to prove his or her competence with content and activities that *go beyond* the curriculum. This is often the difference in the minds of learners of being taught as opposed to being *challenged.*'

'You mean the teacher can't simply present what's in the text?'

'I mean the teacher can't just talk through the material in the text but must perform with tasks and problems that go beyond examples in the text — that challenge students with the world outside the classroom.'

'That sounds like a teacher who must show his or her muscle.'

'Yes, but muscle not just for the sake of muscle — ego inflating maneuvers that may be impressive but tangential to the goals of a lesson. They have to be directed at the same mental processes, activities and responses to be expected of the learners not only at the end of the lesson but in the world outside the classroom. In a sense, demonstrating capability is previewing what the learner can and should be able to do in your classroom *and* in life.'

'That sounds like what Mrs. Davis would say any good coach instinctively would do.'

'You're right, the coach doesn't just talk about the game but throws the ball, swings the bat, demonstrates a tackle, etc., not only to model the behavior but to demonstrate his or her own capability in performing the actions being expected of the players.'

'In classrooms in which capability is rarely shown, students tune out the teacher just as they would tune out any peer they believe doesn't show the capability to back up his or her words with real actions and deeds. This is the world students live in and come to respect in as well as out of the classroom.'

'It seems that in many classrooms we mistake talking for doing.'

'Yes, in some classrooms a recitation of rules, regurgitating the text, carrying out procedures, and even working through examples in a workbook substitute for demonstrating a teacher's capability in a more real, lifelike and authentic environment. This calls for stretching yourself beyond the immediate confines of the text or workbook to perform the complex actions, problem solving activities and decisions required not only at the end of a lesson but in the world outside the classroom. It means not "hiding behind" exercises the students may be expected to complete but going beyond them to create lifelike and challenging problems that require a high and refined level of performance.'

'But, how does a teacher show capability?'

'One way is to go beyond the presentation of content to show its implications. Implications provide the opportunity to ask higher level questions that may not always be obvious to the student.'

'You mean by posing questions that encourage higher level thinking — like problem-solving and decision-making?'

'Yes. With implication questions the teacher demonstrates and models the higher mental processes that students are expected to use outside the classroom.'

'In many classrooms situation and problem questions won't be enough to get students committed to the goals of your lesson. Then, *implication questions* become important.'

'Can you give me some examples of implication questions?'

'For example,

> If you didn't use an apostrophe to denote possession, *what would be* some errors in interpretation that would be made?
> If the temperature were raised in a chamber containing air and gasoline, *what would happen*?
> If the development of tools necessary to make boats and a knowledge of navigation didn't exist, *how could* our earliest ancestors have traveled across continents?
> *What would you* predict would happen in a democracy without laws?

Each of these go beyond the presentation of content to force an understanding of the implications of content in the real-world. They challenge the learner to make predictions, generalizations and discriminations that require higher level thinking — just the kind you and I make in our everyday lives.'

'Are there still other types of questions?'

'The last step to successful lessons in large heterogeneous classrooms is obtaining a *commitment to learn*. This step can't be achieved if the teacher doesn't first set a decision-making tone, establish a need, and demonstrate his or her capability.'

'You mean the teacher can't assume there is a commitment to learn before all of this is done?'

'Not only a commitment to learn can't be assumed, but even a willingness to respond can't be assumed. Learners in large heterogeneous classes are more prone not to respond at all than in small homogeneous classes. The accumulative strength of numbers, a rejection of the structure and routine of the classroom, hiding behind the responses of a few, and the independence and willfulness which comes from the presence of different value systems all may be part of the increasing number of "I don't know" responses or lack of responses being found in classrooms today.'

'So, are you saying the most immediate problem in some classes may not be to get learners to respond correctly but to get them to respond at all?'

'I'm saying that a commitment to learn must be connected to a payoff for the learner which he or she truly values in order for a thoughtful response to be made.'

'Like a reward of some kind?'

'Not exactly. In heterogeneous classrooms, the successful teachers I know work from a different perspective. First, these teachers are realistic enough to know that any amount of reinforcement — for example, learn it well and we'll skip the homework, or you'll need this skill on any job — won't be sufficient to get and keep many of today's students committed to learning. The world outside school is far too glamorous — filled with "real" rewards — for anything inside the classroom to pose serious competition.'

'So what kind of reward are you talking about?'

'Effective teachers take a different path to obtaining a commitment to learn. For them a commitment to learn means obtaining a commitment to resolve a problem that their students see important, if not in their own lives, then, in the lives of others — that's the payoff and the reward.'

'But, how do you get them to see a problem that's important in their own lives or the lives of others?'

'By posing a problem in a way that can be *resolved* by your students *in the context of your own classroom.*'

'You're saying that successful teachers in heterogeneous classrooms obtain commitment from their students by letting them pose their own solutions to problems?'

'That's right.'

'But, how do you get them to do that?'

'With pay-off questions.'

'What are pay-off questions?'

'*Pay-off questions* naturally follow from implication and problem questions to focus the learners' attention on solutions and actions. They get learners telling *you* the benefits of a desired course of action. One of their most important benefits is that they increase the acceptability and credibility of what you are teaching to learners. Since they encourage students to focus on solutions and the benefits solutions would bring, they link content to a purpose which is meaningful in the eyes of your students.'

'Can you give some examples of pay-off questions?'

'For example,

How could a rule be formed *to distinguish* the proper name, "Burns" from the proper name "Burn", for whom we want to show possession?

How might the amount of fuel, air and temperature be controlled in an automobile in *the right amounts* to create safe and efficient combustion?

What kind of climate would you create during earlier times that would allow our earliest ancestors to *travel between continents*?

How would a government be formed that would give all of its citizens the right to be free but *not to do as they please*?

Each of these pay-off questions ask the students to provide a solution to a situation, need and implication established in earlier questions.'

'Let me see if I understand. Pay-off questions focus the learners' attention on a solution rather than a problem.'

'You've got it. Pay-off questions change the classroom from a *problem discovery* climate to a *problem solving* climate.'

'Do you think anyone could use pay-off questions to teach in a classroom with many different learning needs?'

'If first they'd establish a decision-making climate, identify a need, and demonstrate capability, I'm sure they'd be effective.'

Reflections

1 Contrast a typical lesson plan with the approach used by Mr. Koker to teach a heterogeneous class of learners. What are the steps in each of these approaches?

2 How would Mr. Koker characterize the behavior of learners in a large heterogeneous classroom at the start of a lesson? What does he recommend a teacher do at the start of a lesson?

3 Using a topic from your teaching field, formulate a situation, problem, implication, and pay-off question.

4 What is Mr. Koker's idea of a reward that can elicit from students a commitment to learn? Give an example of this kind of reward — or pay-off.

5 Contrast the role of the teacher in making content relevant to a small class of homogeneous learners who share similar abilities, learning histories and value systems, with that of a large class of heterogeneous learners.

Field Activity

Identify in the boxes below an actual classroom example that you have observed of a *situation, problem, implication*, and *pay-off* question.

Situation:

Problem:

Implication:

Pay-off:

12   Becoming a Leader

By this time she felt she had discovered a lot about effective schools and effective teaching and it was time to bring her visits to a close. As she turned toward the principal's office to share what she had learned, a sign over the teachers' lounge caught her attention. It read '1 per cent of all leaders are born, the other 99 percent earn it.'

'What an odd place', she thought, 'to see a sign about leaders. This was a place for teachers — not politicians, business executives, or school administrators.' She wondered if in all her discussions she had missed something. Curious, she opened the door to find several teachers talking.

'I'm sorry to bother you, but I'm the journalist doing the story on effective teaching. I was just passing by when I noticed the sign on the door. I'm afraid in my visits with other teachers no one mentioned the word "leader" and I was wondering what it meant.'

'Well, I'm Mr. Barkley, and I'm afraid you may have missed something.'

'I'd like to know what it is.'

'If you're not a leader you're not an effective teacher.'

'Why is that?'

'Because if you're not a leader you really can't do all the other things you've been learning about and you can't inspire others to do them.'

'You mean part of a teacher's job is to *inspire other teachers?*'

'How do you think this school got the reputation it has? That couldn't happen if everyone only cared about themselves — never communicating to others the things that made them effective.'

'That explains why some of the teachers I met talked about the same things. They must have passed on to others what they discovered for themselves'

'Of course. Leadership is sharing a common set of experiences. In this school we share what is effective and each of us brings our own special discoveries to those around us.'

'*Who* are the leaders in a school like this, and what characteristics do they have?'

'The first question is easy. We all are leaders — or working to become leaders. The second question is more difficult. I think we could name quite a few things that make a teacher a leader.'

'Could you give me an idea of what kinds of things?'

'Well, I can give you one. Leaders — the ones who are truly effective — have a purpose for teaching that expresses who they are.'

'That's one of the characteristics Ms. Beecham spoke about. But, how does that relate to leadership?'

'Those teachers who have a purpose for teaching show to others around them a style and personality that is distinctively their own. It's not that others necessarily will admire the unique purpose which they have chosen, but that they have a purpose at all.'

'So, you're saying someone who feels strongly about something and backs up his or her feelings with conviction is a leader?'

'That's part of it. Others become attracted to someone like that. They might even ask "Why does she have such a strong belief? What makes him work so hard? How does she keep going?" Underneath the question is a silent admiration.'

'But, don't those questions suggest that someone is giving more to the system than could ever be given back to them?'

'The teachers who have a purpose and conviction never chose it with the expectation that recognition or reward would be forthcoming. They chose it for themselves to see and to enjoy.'

'You mean their purpose becomes a source of inspiration for themselves.'

'And for others. Others see someone enjoying the same job that they do and can't help but be amazed how they do it. They observe carefully, half disbelieving what they see and half wanting to feel the same excitement and enjoyment.'

'In other words, you're saying having a purpose is contagious.'

'Yes. It's a source of meaning for others who may have lost

their own sense of purpose. Seeing it in another, they grow to admire it for themselves and, eventually, search for it themselves.'

'Could you give me another characteristic of an effective leader?'

'I bet Mrs. Cornell, over there, could.'

'Well, I've been listening and I'd say believing in yourself would be another mark of a leader. Hopefully, a spouse, loved one, or close friend will believe in you, but that's no guarantee their confidence will transfer to your classroom at the time you most need it. Leaders — those who are most influential in the lives of others around them — have confidence — a belief in themselves. They're able to see themselves apart from the good/ bad, right/wrong value judgments that others so often place on themselves.'

'That's an interesting point because Mrs. Davis spoke to me about something very much like that. Teachers who are leaders are like dispassionate umpires at their own game, she might say.'

'That's right. To them events that happen in their classrooms are simply "hits" and "misses". A miss — at handling Johnny's misbehavior, at making quadratic equations understandable, at showing competence before the class in forming possessives, or in gaining the confidence of slow learners — is simply an event that happened — and that now can be *changed*. In fact, for these leaders there are only near misses, since every event that occurs is an opportunity to change things for the better the next time around.'

'What you seem to be describing is the positive outlook that a leader places on things gone wrong.'

'And what becomes a source of admiration to others is not simply a belief in oneself when things go wrong but the tangible rewards it brings in improving your own performance — and the performance of others who may be watching.'

'And there's the leadership again.'

'Yes. A belief in oneself makes one try harder than anyone else — and trying harder brings results. That — not a flawless performance — is what is so admired by others who are watching. Here comes Mr. Thomson — maybe he has something to add?'

'How can I help?'

'I was just talking with Mrs. Cornell and before that Mr. Barkley about characteristics of effective leaders. I'm afraid the sign over the door caught my attention. They told me leaders have a purpose for teaching and a belief in themselves. But, are there any other characteristics that make a teacher a leader?'

'Teachers who are leaders are student focused.'

'But, if students aren't the focus of a teacher's attention, what is?'

'Oh, you'd be surprised. For a lot of teachers, especially new teachers, their focus is exclusively on themselves or the mechanics of teaching. They or their teaching materials are always at the center of their attention. It's as though for them teaching is simply the task of managing their own behavior and that of their instructional materials. To make improvements in either area is to them all that's needed to be a success. And, of course, they strive to get better and better at it without much notice as to what the effects of these so-called improvements are on their learners.'

'That sounds a lot like the stages of concerns Mrs. Thomas was telling me about.'

'We've all seen them — especially in less experienced teachers.'

'But, is a concern for one's own survival and the materials and activities of the teaching task really all that bad?'

'You're right in that we all are concerned about our own survival and the mechanics of teaching. It's the exclusiveness of one's focus on those concerns as opposed to their effects on students that drains you of valuable energy that can leave you without any other goal.'

'Now I'm beginning to see what Mrs. Thomas was talking about.'

'All teachers, at some time and to some degree, will be concerned with their own survival in front of a class and with their materials and lesson plans. But, an exclusive focus on either, which can sometimes consume the beginning teacher, shifts their attention away from student learning.'

'But it would seem that a concern for self and the teaching task are ways any new teacher must learn how to teach.'

'You're right, but it doesn't have to be that way when you focus on what your students are learning. When that happens you find you no longer need to focus on yourself *or* the teaching task. Your instruction is guided by your impact on learners and that impact creates a confidence that no longer requires an exclusive focus on your own survival.'

'So, is a teacher who is student focused noticed by other teachers more than, say, someone who is concerned exclusively with self or the teaching task?'

'You bet. A student focus provides a direction for not just where others should be going but where they want to go. Student focused teachers inevitably become models for those who want to attain a higher level of professional concern and commitment.'

'Are there other characteristics of leaders I should know about?'

'Maybe Mrs. Hensley over there might have some.'

'Well, I've heard what you've been saying, and I'd have to add that another characteristic of teachers who are leaders is that they actively seek out relationships with other professionals.'

'You mean they make friends?'

'Not just friends but colleagues who can identify with their purpose for teaching and with whom they share something in common.'

'Could you explain?'

'Well, they form networks with other teachers according to some mutual purpose. In other words, those comprising the network know exactly why it exists — why they have agreed to come together as friends as well as colleagues.'

'You mean to share visuals, handouts or lesson plans — things like that?'

'Yes, but they also come together for even broader goals like to decide how to remediate arithmetic errors or to make grammar and spelling lessons more relevant for certain types of learners.'

'So, I guess what you're saying is that networks need to fulfill some instructional need that's common among those who join them?'

'But, not all networks need to be centered around instructional tasks. They can also represent concerns about classroom management, school rules, clerical duties, in-service requirements and even provide emotional support to one another.'

'In each case, though, you're saying a network of interested teachers comes together to meet a need that's in common.'

'That's right but within the limited time and resources of all its members.'

'Now I see why you call them leaders — they are network builders — they create relationships between who has what and who needs what — with themselves in the middle. But what about their own needs?'

'They get out of the network just what everyone else gets out of it, no more, no less. In other words, they aren't disinterested matchmakers who don't share in the rewards of the network.'

'So, a network has to have the capacity to serve all its members.'

'That's right and that can be a very difficult part of building networks.'

'Why?'

'Because networks can easily serve some members more than others, sometimes resulting in jealousy and resentment toward those who gain the most.'

'I guess you're saying networks in which all the members don't derive some benefit won't last very long.'

'. . . or exist in name only. And that is where leadership skills in creating a network count the most. If the network is built only on the needs of the network initiator — more than likely there will be no network at all. If it is built on the needs of only a select few who consistently utilize the resources of others, resentment and eventual abandonment of the network results.'

'So, the key is to form networks for topics which fulfill a common purpose and to select network participants who have comparable amounts of time, energy and resources to devote to the network.'

'That's right. Leaders are at the hub of many different networks, giving and taking about equally from each.'

'Now I see why leaders are also effective teachers — they have at their disposal the resources of many other teachers and aren't afraid to invest their time to form partnerships that can make their own teaching better.'

'You've got it.'

'Hi, I'm Martha, and I'd like to add something.'

'I'd like to hear it.'

'In my opinion, leaders are also innovators — artists at changing and thinking flexibly — coming up with fresh ideas and taking advantage of unexpected events.'

'Such as . . .'

'Things that happen right in front of you every day that can be turned around by changing the way you do something — maybe even only a little.'

'Well, that's interesting, because I recall Mr. Koker saying that creativity in teaching doesn't mean big changes that come from outside your classroom. The creativity that effects your teaching the most and lasts the longest represents little changes that come from what you do or change in your own classroom.'

'That's right. They are changes in how you think about something that maybe you did the same way for years but somehow now manage to do differently. The creativity I'm talking about is small in comparison to anything that would capture the attention of large numbers of people — it costs little in time or energy and is effective because it comes from your own classroom.'

'So how do you become creative?'

'First, it requires a teacher that's at the highest level of professional concern.'

'You mean a concern for the impact you're having on your students' learning?'

'That's right. It requires you to be in touch with your students and your impact on them — your actions and their reactions.'

'Ms. Davis was saying how important it was to be aware of your own behavior. Is that part of it?'

'Yes. So that you know what to change when it needs to be changed. You are observing yourself, so to speak, always in touch with what you're doing and what your students' reactions are to what you're doing.'

'Ms. Davis told me that that would only be possible if you lay to rest critical self-judgment. Then, you can be more aware of your own behavior and your feelings about it. Is that part of it?'

'It's the way rapid and flexible responses are made. There are no "rights" or "wrongs" — only things that should be changed or could be made better another time. Casting aside critical self-judgment gives you the opportunity to see your own behavior and to feel your actions — what feels natural — unhampered by what others or even your own critical self might think.'

'Could that be why a focus on student impact is so important? — it takes our attention off that part of us that critically judges what we do — at the time we're doing it.'

'Exactly. Teachers who are aware of their own behavior and are sensitive to their feelings are the most likely to meet the learning needs of their students. Not coincidentally, these teachers are also those who have a purpose for teaching that makes them most concerned about their impact on students.'

'Your notion of creativity seems to be at the heart of a lot of what I've been hearing.'

'And, what's that?'

'How to be flexible — to change and adapt to make an impact on students.'

'That's right. Creativity is being able to create an endless variety of responses to conditions you could not anticipate.'

'I remember Mr. Koker speaking about that — how important it is that a teacher be able to create responses that match the variety of reactions coming from your students. He called it "flow". So, what he really was describing was the ability of a teacher to be creative — to create patterns of responses that they may never have seen before. That's when you become student-focused.'

'That's right. You have the ability to create new and flexible responses that match the needs of your learners, because you have a concern for your impact on students. That's a concern that doesn't go unnoticed.'

'You mean by other teachers?'

'Yes. They look and listen and take for themselves what may be valuable for their own classrooms. Call them little nuggets of ingenuity, tips or best practices — they are what other teachers search for in their peers.'

'How do others find out about them?'

'Not perhaps in the way you think. Leaders don't always teach these nuggets of ingenuity, tips or best practices to others — they allow them to come to the attention of others.'

'How?'

'By talking freely about life in their classroom — telling

stories and anecdotes about what happened to them in class, and sharing their experiences with networks of friends and colleagues. This is the way creativity of the best kind gets communicated and shared.'

'I'm glad I stopped in. Now I feel I'm ready to write my story and to thank the principal for the opportunity of meeting so many interesting — and effective — teachers.'

Reflections

1   According to the dialogue, what five leadership characteristics do effective teachers possess? What do you believe are the most important for a beginning teacher in the first weeks of school?

2   How would you account for the fact that having a purpose for teaching that expresses who you are often inspires other teachers to find a purpose of their own?

3   Can you explain why having confidence and acquiring a belief in yourself is important to being able to adapt to the changing conditions of the classroom?

4   How does reaching the highest stage of professional concern — a concern for your impact on students — help curtail the disruptive influence of Self 1 and acquire new patterns of behavior?

5   Provide an example of a peer network in your grade or content area that has the capacity to serve all its members equally. Indicate the individual responsibilities of several teachers, how often and where you would meet, and how the information gathered would be exchanged.

Field Activity

Indicate in the boxes below four 'nuggets of ingenuity', professional 'tips' or best practices that have come to your attention through a real-life story or anecdote revealed by a teacher. What was the nature of the story that became the vehicle by which the practice was made known to others?

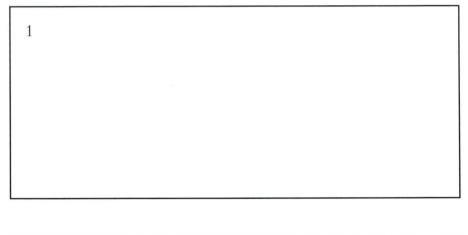

1

2

3

4

Effective Teachers: Annotated Readings

BERLINER, D.C. (1987) 'Ways of thinking about students and classrooms by more and less experienced teachers' in CALDERHEAD, J. (Ed.) *Exploring Teacher's Thinking*, London, Cassell Educational Limited, pp. 60–83.

> This article examines the professional expertise of teachers by studying the differences in how knowledge is used by experienced teachers who were judged to be expert, novice teachers who were pre-service or first year teachers, and teachers-to-be who had high levels of subject matter knowledge but no classroom experience. The author describes how these groups see and reflect upon knowledge of the classroom differently and what types of knowledge and reflection are most typical of expert teachers (dialogues 8 and 10).

BOLIN, F.S. (1988) 'Helping student teachers think about teaching', *Journal of Teacher Education*, **39,** 2, pp. 48–54.

> The author describes how student teachers develop a concept of teaching and think about their role as teachers. Through a case study of one pre-service teacher's journal entries and interviews with a university supervisor, the author describes stages of development and the role of self-awareness and reflection in becoming an effective teacher (dialogues 8 and 10).

GORE, J. (1987) 'Reflecting in reflective teaching', *Journal of Teacher Education*, March-April, pp. 33–9.

> This article defines and then explores some of the advantages and disadvantages of current definitions of reflective teaching. The author compares and contrasts an analytical approach to self-observation and reflective teaching with a popular task-oriented approach (dialogue 8).

GREEN, M. (1986) 'Perspectives and imperatives: Reflection and passion in teaching', *Journal of Curriculum and Supervision*, **3**, 2, pp. 109–20.

> This article conveys an impassioned plea for teachers to open themselves to the power of possibility — to think, to be mindful, to reach beyond — to reconceptualize their classroom and everyday actions. The author describes the important role of the human traits of tacit knowing, insight and intuitive awareness in becoming an effective teacher (dialogues 7–10).

GROSSMAN, P.A., WILSON, S. and SHULMAN, L.S. (1989) 'Teachers of substance: Subject matter knowledge for teaching' in REYNOLDS, M.C. (Ed.) *Knowledge Base for Beginning Teachers*, New York, Pergamon Press.

> This article explains that one of the first challenges facing beginning teachers is the transformation of their subject matter knowledge into a form that is relevant to students and specific to the task of teaching. The authors identify and illustrate several practical ways teachers can make this transformation (dialogue 11).

KAGAN, D.M. (1989) 'The heuristic value of regarding classroom instruction as an aesthetic medium', *Educational Researcher*, **18**, 6, pp. 11–18.

> This article explains how a lesson can be more than the content it conveys. Using the notions of symmetry, balance and parsimony, the author illustrates how effective teachers plan lessons that help learners interpret and retain lesson content that is presented as a performance, a message and a work of art (dialogue 9).

LIVINGSTON, C. and BORKO, H. (1989) 'Expert-novice differences in teaching: A cognitive analysis and implications for teacher education', *Journal of Teacher Education*, July-August, pp. 36–42.

> The authors describe an investigation of the thoughts and actions of a small number of expert and novice teachers. The article presents differences between teachers' performance from two perspectives — teaching as a cognitive skill and

teaching as an improvisational performance — and in so doing make the distinction between thinking and doing (dialogue 8).

WILSON, S.M., SHULMAN, L.S. and RICHERT, A.E. (1987) '150 different ways of knowing: Representations of knowledge in teaching' in CALDERHEAD, J. (Ed.) (1987) *Exploring Teachers' Thinking*, London, Cassell, pp. 104–24.
    The authors follow a group of beginning teachers through their professional training and into their first year of teaching to examine how their subject matter knowledge is translated into classroom practice. They illustrate the important role of analogies, explanations and examples, and the teachers' own critical reflection in communicating subject matter effectively (dialogue 8).

Part III:

Effectiveness Revisited

13   Looking Back

*She walked slowly toward the principal's office thinking about all she had heard. She tried organizing her thoughts as she had before. But, this time it seemed harder. There were no facts to memorize or notes to help her — only things to think about. The more she thought the more she realized that what she really had learned from her visits was not how **to be** an effective teacher, but how **to become** an effective teacher. She learned what old mental habits had to be discarded and what new ones had to be acquired, if a teacher was to be truly effective.*

As she approached the door to the principal's office, she decided to put into practice some of what she had heard. She would dispel her old mental habit of being fearful of what the principal might think — what she might have expected her to learn and maybe didn't. She decided to subdue the critical self-judgments she was already making at the hands of Self 1 and to be in touch with her feelings — what she really felt and discovered. With a renewed commitment to put some old mental habits aside, she knocked on the principal's door one last time.

'I've heard you've been asking some pretty important questions. Does this visit mean you're about finished?'

'I am.'

'So, tell me what you've learned.'

'Well, I'm afraid it's not so easy. You see, I found that effective teaching is a lot more than I'd expected.'

'And, what did you expect?'

'I expected to learn how teachers prepared their lessons, wrote objectives, selected materials, determined grades, made tests — the things they spend a lot of their time doing. But, that's not what really makes the difference. It's how you put ordinary skills and competencies together into something bigger — not just to get through a lesson or unit but to get through it in a way that

has an impact on student learning and growth that can't always be measured at the end of the lesson or unit. That's where a teacher's *attitude* comes in.'

'Such as.'

How you choose to see things — whether you see your students' potential to learn and to grow as half-empty or half-full,

How aware you are of yourself — how conscious you are of your own behavior at the time you're teaching, and

What you value — if you have a purpose for teaching that's more than just presenting content?'

'How do these things make a difference?'

'Well, just as you happen to have shared with me some characteristics of an effective school, I can share with you some of the characteristics of effective teachers that I discovered.'

'So what did you discover?'

'One thing I discovered is that effective teachers have a purpose for teaching that's more than simply presenting content. They've discovered for themselves who they really are that can make their teaching fresh and exciting each day.'

'You mean they mix duty and pleasure.'

'I mean, they teach but have fun doing it.'

'How?'

'By relating their teaching to something inside themselves — what they really believe in and stand for.'

'You mean they change what they teach to suit themselves?'

'No. They find ways in which the curriculum can be extended, reinforced and made relevant by who they are and what they believe in. For example, Mrs. Beecham asked me to make a list of my own deep convictions, things I believe in and would fight tooth and nail for.'

'And could you?'

'Not at first. It was hard because I kept repeating what I thought everyone else wanted me to believe in. Like coming here, I thought about what you might want me to say.'

'Were you finally able to make a list?'

'Yes, I found lots of things that both make me distinctive and that could be used to make any job more interesting and exciting — more a part of myself.'

'Such as . . .'

'For example, I realized how much I like to analyze why people behave the way they do, how much I like people who aren't afraid to share their feelings, and that some of the most important things in life we have to do ourselves. Now, I can think of a lot of ways I can convey these values in the stories I write and at the same time make my job more relevant and exciting. And, so could any teacher.'

'But, first, you have to find what you believe in.'

'That's right. That's how Mrs. Beecham helped me. I created my own list of things I believe in.'

'Anything else?'

'Then I discovered that effective teachers don't think in terms of "right" or "wrong".'

'I'm not sure I understand.'

'To be effective you have to think about *success* and *failure* differently. For example, take the goal of getting to the end of the lesson before time is up, or teaching learners the fundamentals on which you're going to base your next lesson, or getting the class to behave.'

'I don't see anything wrong with those goals.'

'There isn't, but because you've learned to expect those consequences — the lesson finished on time, all your learners grasp the fundamentals, the class behaves — you think you've failed when they don't occur. Those are just events that happened — they're neither good nor bad until someone says they are. They're value judgments that have been made outside your classroom before the event took place — in your past, a textbook you read, or a student teaching experience. They represent what Ms. Davis calls Self 1 — that side of us that tells us to expect consequences learned at another time and criticizes us if they don't occur. That's what creates the sense of failure Ms. Davis sees in some of her student teachers.'

'So, what's the answer?'

'It lies in being aware of your own behavior at the time you're teaching and changing it when necessary. If you're worrying about your success or failure, you can't be aware of your own behavior.'

'I think I see your point. A lot of new teachers I observe are so anxious they can't recall their own behavior.'

'And being aware of your own behavior is important because that's when you're most able to change the course of events — choose new responses that may never have been chosen before.'

'You mean you're more able to be flexible and adapt to the changing conditions of the classroom.'

'That's right. The consequence you had anticipated may *never* occur — because classrooms are too unpredictable for that, Ms. Davis would say. That's why expecting learned consequences as a sign of your success could be dangerous for a new teacher, any teacher — since they don't happen all that often due to the fast-paced and unpredictable nature of classrooms. Those consequences which stick to us as images in our heads come from somewhere outside the classroom at another time or place.'

'So, what can a teacher do?'

'Ms. Davis would say place Self 2 in command of the show.'

'What's that mean?'

'I think it means that once you believe learned consequences no longer need to occur, you become more aware of your own behavior — since you're looking inward — toward yourself — not outward toward what someone else may think or feel — and, so, you're free to create new and creative responses that are more responsive to the conditions around you. You produce a new response rather than expect an old one.'

'Does that mean you can't fail?'

'In a manner of speaking. You have near misses — events that may not have worked the way you wanted but that now can be changed — and, then, changed again.'

'Are there any other characteristics of an effective teacher?'

'Mr. Koker believes that effective teachers have something called, flow. That's an ability to link your feelings with what's happening at the moment to create new responses to unanticipated events. It's a way of describing how a teacher responds in a classroom in which the effects of a lot of what you do are unpredictable and previously learned consequences don't always happen.'

'And, what do effective teachers do?'

'They change the script or program they've become accustomed to. What I learned from Mr. Koker is that for the less effective teacher:

learned consequences are matched with present conditions to produce a response that is a success if the expected consequences occur and a failure if they don't.'

'And, what do effective teachers do?'

'Since effective teachers don't anticipate previously learned consequences, they are more likely to be

aware of their own behavior and their feelings of comfort or discomfort from which they choose a new response to meet the changing conditions before them.'

'That sounds like effective teachers become aware of their mistakes and learn from them.'

'Both Mrs. Beecham and Mr. Koker seem to say it's what every teacher who wants to be effective has to do. They have to set aside the expectation that previously learned consequences will or even have to occur for their actions to be a success. That, in turn, frees them to become more aware — conscious you might say — of their own behavior and their feelings of comfort or discomfort with it. Then, they can respond with new behaviors for which they may have no previously learned consequences and, therefore, no fear of trying something new.'

'In other words, they're continuously writing their own script or program.'

'That's what Mr. Koker would say flow is all about — creating your own script to respond to the fast pace of events unfolding before you.'

'I think you've gotten a pretty good picture of an effective teacher. Are there any other characteristics?'

'Yes, and it follows from what the others have said. That was one of the nice things about my visits with your teachers; they seemed to be saying many of the same things in different ways.'

'What did they say?'

'Mrs. Thomas told me about the stages of concern most teachers go through on the way to becoming effective. They're what you're most concerned about and focus on at different times of your career.'

'I know that most teachers change in pretty predictable ways.'

'Then, you'd recognize the stages Mrs. Thomas told me about.'

'What are they?'

'The first is a concern for your own survival — getting through the day without losing your wits or the class getting out of control. It's when all your energy is directed to protecting your own fragile state of mind.'

'Yes. New teachers haven't gained the confidence yet to think beyond their own survival — getting through the day without embarrassment.'

'That's how Mrs. Thomas and some of the other teachers would describe it. It's a time of insecurity that comes from all of a sudden being confronted with things that never happened to you before.'

'And, that's when a lot of new teachers become self-critical.'

'When they leave those critical self-judgments behind, they can move to the next stage of concern Ms. Thomas told me about.'

'And what's that?'

'It's a concern for the teaching task. It's when the teacher decides to become more sure by organizing himself or herself so that hardly anything can go wrong — or change.'

'I've seen that, too.'

'Mrs. Thomas says to stay survival-oriented for very long is so emotionally exhausting that most teachers move on to this next stage very quickly. It's when their concerns turn almost exclusively to organizing their teaching — handouts, workbooks, and materials — to keep things structured and students busy with the least threat to the orderliness of the classroom.'

'But, some might say, what's wrong with that?'

'That's what I asked Mrs. Thomas. And you know what she said? That it's not your focus on the teaching task that's the problem — since every teacher has to organize themselves for teaching — but the extent to which your focus on the resources and materials of teaching prevents an awareness of the impact you're having on your students.'

'In other words, you're saying that some ways of organizing the teaching task may help one survive but may not help students to learn.'

'That's what Mrs. Thomas would say. Organizing yourself to *protect* the orderliness of the classroom may make your teaching less responsive to the learning needs of your students. From the outside looking in everything's fine, but from the point of view of student learning nothing may be happening.'

'That's what's so hard when I observe my teachers. I'm always on the outside looking in, and so I have to make a lot of judgments about what's going on beneath the surface — whether student learning and growth are really taking place. I think you've made an important distinction. Now, I'm curious. Is there another stage of concern?'

'It follows from what you've been saying.'

'What's that?'

'The third and highest stage of a teacher's development is making instructional decisions based upon a concern for student learning and growth. It's when the teacher's focus turns to his or her impact on students, while balancing these with concerns for their own survival and the teaching task. Now, the teacher is free to change and to create new and flexible responses for the purpose of having an impact on student learning.'

'That sounds like flow, again.'

'It is. You become more in touch with — more aware of — your own behavior when your focus is not exclusively on yourself and the mechanics of teaching. Now you can feel what you're doing — and change to improve your level of comfort based on student learning.'

'Do they go together — level of comfort and student learning?'

'I think the teachers I talked with would say they do. When you're not fearful of expected consequences, you look outward to your students for your comfort zone not inward to yourself. The former is a Stage 3 teacher who derives pleasure from seeing students change as a result of what they're doing — maybe sometimes only in small amounts but change in a desirable direction just the same.'

'You're describing a lot of the teachers in this school. They're always changing what they're doing to increase their effect on learners and keep them moving in the right direction.'

'You would say they're keeping the train on the tracks and headed toward student learning and growth.'

'That's right. If teachers aren't committed to having an impact on their learners — neither the school nor its teachers will be effective. Are there any other characteristics of an effective teacher?'

'Another comes from a visit I had with Mr. Randall.'

'He's one of our new teachers.'

'And, that's why I wanted to see him. To get a fresh perspective from someone who might be struggling with a lot of concerns with self-survival and the teaching task.'

'And, was he?'

'Well, that's an interesting question. I don't think so from what I could tell. He seemed to skip or at least shorten the time spent in those initial stages and already appeared to be thinking of his own behavior in terms of his impact on students.'

'How was that?'

'He told me about an approach that has helped him get a start on some of the problems a teacher has in teaching learners with many different learning needs.'

'You mean he has some special way of teaching heterogeneously grouped learners?'

'He seems to have a way of making his classes exciting and relevant to what's happening in the real world and in the lives of most of his students.'

'How?'

'By recognizing that the formality of a classroom and the structure of the teacher's routine may not be sufficient to obtain a commitment to learn — as it might be in a small class of learners with similar learning histories.'

'What does he do?'

'He recognizes that his learners are decision-makers — capable of making some important decisions about the things they're studying and the world they live in.'

'How?'

'By establishing a climate for decision-making that gives his students the opportunity to think independently and critically. He begins by acknowledging student strengths, telling them what they've learned, accomplished or mastered so far. That gives them the confidence they need to make decisions for themselves and to direct their own learning. He uses something called a situation question to bring out the facts, information or background about a situation which his learners already know something about — then, uses these questions to establish a climate for learning.'

'And, then?'

'He gets learners to perceive the importance of what is about to be taught in terms of their own, not the teacher's world.'

'In other words, he doesn't assume that his learners will think what is about to be taught is important.'

'That's right. Mr. Randall would say that making that assumption can cost a teacher of heterogeneously grouped learners a lot of time. Just because it's in the curriculum doesn't mean the students will see it as something they should learn. Instead, effective teachers of heterogeneous classes work at making the content relevant in the eyes of their learners.'

'How do they do it?'

'By presenting content in the context of problems that relate to real or perceived student needs. Mr. Randall would say, *needs are to learners what objectives are to teachers.*'

'But, how exactly?'

'By posing problem questions to his learners. Problem questions raise difficulties and contradictions that point to a need. They illuminate contradictions or irregularities that call for the creation of a solution, a will to act or change a way of doing things. By accentuating a problem or dilemma, you're telling the students they can find solutions to the problem or resolve the dilemma *within your lesson.*'

'You mean they're beginning to make decisions for themselves — taking control over their own learning because they see it as relevant.'

'I think that's it. It gets the class trying to solve a problem they were led to discover themselves. That raises the excitement of learning and gets the class to voluntarily commit themselves to the goals of the lesson.'

'Are there other steps?'

'In heterogeneous classes where there are many different learning needs, Mr. Randall would say that the teacher must also demonstrate capability. That means going beyond the routine exercises at the end of the chapter to relate what is being learned to the real world. In other words, you can't just teach what's in the text. You have to go beyond it, to perform with authentic tasks and problems that will challenge students in the world outside the classroom.'

'I see his point. You have to learn to use the same mental processes in the classroom that we as adults use outside it. That's why performance assessments — oral assignments, extended writing assignments, discussion and the natural dialogue of the classroom — are so important to an effective classroom. They ask students to perform as they would in the adult world.'

'That's what Mr. Randall believes is the important part of demonstrating capability. The teacher demonstrates before the class the same adult behaviors that the students are expected to perform.'

'And, how does a teacher get students to think like an adult?'

'By raising implication questions. Implications of the problem provide the opportunity to make predictions, generalizations and discriminations that require higher level thinking — just the kind we make in our everyday lives.'

'Any other steps to his approach?'

'There is another. Mr. Randall believes that after a climate for decision-making has been set with situation questions, a need established with problem questions and capability demonstrated with implication questions, then, it's time to obtain a commitment to learn.'

'What does that involve?'

'Getting all students to participate in achieving the goals of the lesson — changing a lot of "I don't knows" or no responses to active involvement with the lesson.'

'But, first there must be a commitment to learn.'

'That's right. And, this is where Mr. Randall tackles the problem. He believes that, before students can commit themselves to learn, they have to see some sort of payoff for themselves.'

'A reward or reinforcement?'

'He believes the typical rewards or reinforcements don't work well in school because they can't compete with more attractive rewards and reinforcements outside of school. Instead, pay-offs in school must represent another type of reward or reinforcement.'

'Such as . . .'

'Such as obtaining a commitment to learn by presenting the opportunity to resolve a problem in your own classroom. You see, they're given the chance to provide their own solutions to a problem that was previously brought to light with an implication question. That's how a commitment to learn is obtained — by giving students back the independence they know they have to make decisions and solve problems that reflect the goals of a lesson. Pay-off questions get learners telling the teacher the benefits of a solution that are meaningful in the eyes of students.'

'Are there any other characteristics of an effective teacher?'

'Just this morning, I discovered one more.'

'What is it?'

'You know the sign over the teacher's lounge?'

'Sure.'

'I poked my head in while Mr. Barkley and Mrs. Cornell were talking and asked what the sign meant. I'm afraid I missed an important point in my visits.'

'What was that?'

'That effective teachers are leaders. Part of their job is to inspire other teachers — to share with others the things that make them effective. That's when I discovered how a lot of the teachers I talked with came to share many of the same ideas.'

'You mean they talked the same language.'

'Yes. Saw things the same or used different words to express the same things. They must have had many of the same experiences and shared them with one another.'

'I think that's one of the most important characteristics I found of an effective school — sharing among teachers.'

'I believe that was one of your points about what makes effective schools — communication among teachers and administrators and among teachers and parents.'

'Yes, but, did you find teachers who are leaders to have any special qualities?'

'None that we haven't already identified. For example, Mr.

Barkley told me leaders have a purpose for teaching that expresses who they are — and that inspire others to find a purpose of their own. And, then, Mrs. Cornell said the teachers who are leaders believe in themselves — so they can change without fear of doing things differently. They can change the script or program to meet the needs of their learners.'

'That sounds like flow again.'

'I think so, because to change you have to stop always anticipating previously learned consequences. Then, you can become aware of your own behavior more easily and its effects on learners.'

'And, that must mean leaders have a concern for their impact on students.'

'That was another characteristic of a teacher who is a leader suggested by Mrs. Thomson. She repeated what teachers who are at the highest level of professional growth do.'

'Which is have a concern for their impact on learners.'

'That's right.'

'Now, Mrs. Hensley added that teachers who are leaders communicate with each other by forming networks and relationships with other teachers. Just as we were saying, they find others to share their insights and experiences with and gain from the insights and experiences of others.'

'I think she was describing some of the networks the teachers have organized in this school. Some provide emotional support, while others find information, share workbooks, and identify classroom activities that can be used in working with certain types of learners.'

'That's the way she described it — the coming together of interested parties that find they have some common need — and this was the important point she stressed — they all share in the rewards of the network equally. Now, Martha added one other characteristic.'

'That must be Martha Robbins, our student teaching supervisor. What did she say?'

'That effective leaders are teachers who are creative — artists at changing and thinking flexibly in order to make an impact on their students. So, you see, we're back to an effective teacher again. I think everyone I visited was trying to tell me that to be an effective teacher you have to be a leader. I didn't see at first how much the words about leadership over the door really fit.'

'I think you've got quite a story and . . . well . . . so have I.'

'Your teachers gave me a very personal look at what being effective really means — one I don't believe many others have seen or read about. They seemed to speak from the heart and the experience of having discovered for themselves what it means to be effective in a language which describes each of their personal journeys toward becoming effective. I was fortunate to have them share it with me. I know your teachers will enjoy reading their story. Thanks for the opportunity of visiting your school and talking with so many interesting people.'

*She left the principal's office thinking about all she had learned and all those she had met. Her idea of effective teaching was evolving and she needed time to sort out how she would place the characteristics of effective teaching in the same personal and unique language of the teachers with whom she had talked. The task she knew would not be easy, since a lot of what she learned could not be said with many of the traditional words and concepts of teaching which readers might expect. One thing, for sure, she had made many friends in her visits from whom she could seek advice and clarification. As she left school, she thought about what the principal had said — about whether a school really was like a train going in one direction but stopping at different stations to accommodate the destination of each of its passengers. Now, she thought to herself, it was the time to choose **her** destination.*

Related Readings

BEY, T.M. and HOLMES, C.T. (Eds) (1990) *Mentoring: Developing Successful New Teachers*, Reston, VA, Association of Teacher Educators.

The authors provide a practical guide to mentoring that reveals the key ingredients of an effective partnership between the beginning and experienced teacher (dialogue 12).

BOLIN, F.S. (1987) 'Reassessment and renewal in teaching' in BOLIN, F.S. and FALK, J.M. (Eds) *Teacher Renewal: Professional Issues, Personal Choices*, New York, Teachers College Press, pp. 6–16.

The author examines what it means to grow and develop as a teacher using poetry, letters and the experiences of teachers to convey what teacher renewal means in every day life (dialogues 7 and 10).

BORICH, G. (1993) *Clearly Outstanding: Making Each Day Count in Your Classroom*, Boston, MA, Allyn and Bacon.

This book portrays through the lives of Angela, a first grade teacher, Kurt, a junior high teacher, and Sheila, a high school teacher, how teachers at different stages of their careers grow from an exclusive concern for self, to a concern for the teaching task to, finally, a concern for their impact on students (dialogues 7–12).

BORKO, H. and SHAVELSON, R.J. (1990) 'Teachers' decision-making' in JONES, B. and IDOLS, L. (Eds) *Dimensions of Thinking and Cognitive Instruction*, New Jersey, Erlbaum.

The authors identify the decisions that teachers make while planning and carrying out instruction using as their guide the latest advances in cognitive psychology (dialogue 8).

CSIKSZENTMIHALYI, M. (1990) *Flow*, New York, HarperCollins.
This book brings the concept of flow to life by describing its research basis and importance in giving our lives and jobs meaning — from the author who brought this concept to our attention (dialogue 9).

DEWEY, J. (1993) *How We Think: A Statement of the Relation of Reflective Thinking to the Educative Process*, Chicago, IL, Henry Regnery Co.
This classic work presents the basis for many of our current notions of reflective teaching, self-awareness and the distinction between Self 1 and Self 2 (dialogues 7 and 8).

DEWEY, J. (1904) 'The relation of theory to practice in education' in MCMURRY, C.A. (Ed.) *The Relation of Theory to Practice in the Education of Teachers* (Third Yearbook of the National Society for the Scientific Study of Education, Part I), Chicago, IL, University of Chicago Press, pp. 9–30.
This early work presents a historically important foundation for understanding the importance of experience in our professional growth and development as teachers (dialogue 10).

FINE, M.J. and CARLSON, C. (1992) *The Handbook of Family-School Intervention*, Boston, MA, Allyn and Bacon.
This text presents a thorough analysis of family-school partnerships and demonstrates the application of practical interventions to solve a wide range of family-school problems (dialogue 6).

GIROUX, H.A. (1988) *Teachers as Intellectuals: Toward a Critical Pedagogy of Learning*, Boston, MA, Bergin and Garvey.
This author offers an inspiring and convincing view of what effective schools and effective teachers can and should be like (dialogues 1–12).

GOLLNICK, D.M. and CHINN, P.C. (1990) *Multicultural Education in a Pluralistic Society* (3rd edn) New York, Macmillan.
The authors present an up-to-date foundation for teaching culturally diverse and heterogeneous learners that requires

the teacher to establish a decision-making context, identify a need, demonstrate capability, and obtain commitment (dialogue 11).

GOODLAD, J. (1990) *Teachers for Our Nation's Schools*, San Francisco, CA, Jossey-Bass Publishers (chapter 6, 'Becoming a teacher', pp. 196–226).

The author presents the results of a nationwide study of teachers which puts into perspective the important relationship between effective teachers and effective schools (dialogues 1–6).

GRANT, C. (Ed.) (1992) *Research and Multicultural Education: From the Margins to the Mainstream*, London, Falmer Press.

This book provides teachers with a wealth of ideas and concepts for teaching in and understanding the culturally diverse and heterogeneous classroom (dialogue 11).

LEIDER, R.J. (1985) *The Power of Purpose*, New York, Ballantine Books.

The author eloquently describes how individuals in all walks of life can and have benefited from the power of purpose (dialogue 7).

MARSH, C. (1992) *Key Concepts for Understanding Curriculum*, London, Falmer Press.

This book provides teachers and school practitioners with access to research and background involving thirty contemporary issues affecting schools, including the topics of teacher empowerment, leadership, appraisal and curriculum reform (dialogues 1, 5, 12).

PETERSON, P.L. and COMEAUX, M.A. (1987) 'Teachers' schemata for classroom events: The mental scaffolding of teachers' thinking during classroom instruction', *Teaching and Teacher Education*, **3**, pp. 319–31.

This article reports the results of a study that suggests how teachers use different cognitive approaches to think about their instructional roles, organize their subject matter and make instructional decisions rapidly and effectively (dialogues 8 and 10).

REYNOLDS, M.C. (Ed.) (1989) *Knowledge Base for the Beginning Teacher*, New York, Permagon Press.
This edited work presents many well-known authors explaining the important role of subject matter competence and being able to use it to show capability (dialogue 11).

ROGAN, J., BORICH, G. and TAYLOR, H. (1992) 'Validation of stages of concern', *Action in Teacher Education*, summer, **XIV**, 2, pp. 43–9.
This article describes a research study that validates three stages of teacher growth — concern for self, concern for task and concern for student impact — which influence if and how quickly a teacher moves from being a novice to a professional (dialogue 10).

RUSSELL, T. and MUNBY, H. (Eds) (1992) *Teachers and Teaching: From Classroom to Reflection*, London, Falmer Press.
Through case studies, narratives and action research, the authors describe how self-reflection can be put into practice in the classroom to improve one's teaching (dialogue 8).

TABACHNICK, B. and ZEICHNER, K. (Eds) (1991) *Issues and Practices in Inquiry-Oriented Teacher Education*, London, Falmer Press.
The authors explore various examples of reflective teaching in which pre-service student teachers learn to become inquiry-oriented and reflective about their classrooms (dialogues 7–12).

Teachers' Aspiration for School Improvement: A Participatory Decision-Making Workshop. Facilitator's Manual, Facilitator's Manual (1990) Southeastern Educational Improvement Lab, Research Triangle Park, NC.
This manual presents guidelines for a teacher workshop on participative decision making that can result in a school improvement plan based upon consensus among teachers and administrators (dialogue 5).

WEBB, R. (Ed.) (1990) *Practitioner Research in the Primary School*, London, Falmer Press.
  This book provides models and actual examples of how teachers can become practitioner-researchers in their own classrooms and, in the process, acquire a capacity for guiding their own professional development (dialogue 10).

YAXLEY, B. (1991) *Developing Teachers' Theories of Teaching: A Touchstone Approach*, London, Falmer Press.
  The author describes how teachers develop — personally and professionally — by describing a program that helped teachers and teacher educators critically reflect upon their own behavior.

ZEICHNER, K. and LISTON, D. (1987) 'Teaching student teachers to reflect', *Harvard Educational Review*, **57**, pp. 23–8.
  The authors describe an alternative model of teacher training that stimulates self-growth, encourages reflective teaching, greater teacher autonomy, and increased participation in their own governance (dialogues 5, 8, 10).

Index